Contents

Desserts

Seasonal

About Me

A little over 5 years ago, I was getting bored of eating the same things over and over. I think we've all fallen into that trap before haven't we? So I made a vow to attempt at least one new recipe every week. To start with, I'll be honest, it was a little overwhelming. Many meals turned into dinner for the bin & a takeaway for me and the Mr! After a while though, I started to really enjoy it. So much so that the Mr suggested I start a food blog. So that's what I did! And Kitchen Mason was born.

My family still can't quite believe I am this involved with food. I was such a fussy eater as a child! With that being said though, I really used to enjoy baking when I was younger. And what were my go to recipes of choice? The easy to follow step by step kind of course! I knew straight away that was exactly how I wanted to share my recipes with you lovely lot.

So I sincerely hope you love the first Kitchen Mason cook book and the delightful mixture of recipes within. It contains some of the most popular Kitchen Mason recipes and some brand new & exclusive ones just for you. I would also like to say a huge thank you for joining me on my foodie adventures over the years. Whether it's on social media, kitchenmason.com or both, I hope you'll stick around for many more recipes to come.

I would also like to take this opportunity to thank my family and friends for constantly sharing the calories with me & doing a great job of taste testing! (Not that I hear any of you complaining...) With special thanks to 'The Mums' who are always very supportive and honest with their yummy noises!

And of course, the biggest thank you of all goes to the Mr. Without you none of this would even exist. I love you more than words can say.

I hope you enjoy the book my lovelies, until next time!

Emma
(Miss KitchenMason)

Stay In Touch: Website: www.kitchenmason.com Facebook: KitchenMason
Twitter: @KitchenMason Instagram: @KitchenMason Pinterest: KitchenMason

Starters

Cajun Bean Dip with Cheesy Nachos

Caramelised Onion & Rosemary Quiche

Cheese Puffs with Fiery Tomato Salsa

Chorizo Scallops

"Eggs & Cheese"

Garlic & Thyme Baked Camembert

Ham & Cheese Pinwheels

Healthy Pitta "Pizzas"

Posh Cheese & Onion Tarts

Sweet Potato & Cumin Soup

Tomato & Rocket Salad

Starters

Cajun Bean Dip with Cheesy Nachos

This is a fantastic little recipe. Not only is it super healthy but it's perfect for a sharing starter! Easy to make & fun to eat, this is a recipe I guarantee you'll come back to. Want another great perk? You can freeze whatever you don't eat. Waste not want not! Here is what you will need to serve 4 – 6.

- 1 tbsp Garlic Infused Olive Oil
- 1 Onion, **diced**
- 1 tsp Brown Sugar
- 1 tsp White Wine Vinegar
- 1 tsp Cajun Seasoning
- 200g Tin of Mixed Beans, **drained**
- 200g Tin of Cannellini Beans, **drained**
- 400g Tin of Chopped Tomatoes with Herbs
- 200g Bag of Tortilla Chips
- 50g Grated Cheddar/Mozzarella Cheese
- ½ an Avocado, **peeled & cubed (optional)**
- 1 tbsp Fresh Coriander, **chopped (optional)**

Preheat your oven to 190°C/Fan 180°C.
Place a large, non-stick frying pan over a medium heat then add the oil.
Tip the onion into the pan and cook for about 5 minutes until softened.

Add the brown sugar, white wine vinegar & cajun seasoning and continue to cook for 1 minute whilst stirring constantly.

Then add the drained beans & tinned tomatoes. Bring to the boil then reduce to a simmer.

Cook for about 15 minutes, stirring occasionally, until the dip is nice and thick.

Meanwhile, tip the tortilla chips into an ovenproof dish and scatter with the grated cheese. Place into the oven for 5 – 10 minutes until the cheese is just melted.

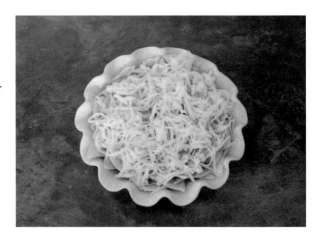

Season the dip to taste with salt and pepper then serve alongside the cheesy tortilla chips. Top with chopped avocado and coriander for an extra fresh taste.

Dig in!

Caramelised Onion & Rosemary Quiche

I love a good quiche. Nothing beats it when you're out on a picnic or enjoying an evening meal in the garden. It's perfect for lunch, dinner, starters, packed lunches or even the dish you take to your friend's Summer BBQ. Always guaranteed to be a hit! So here is what you will need to make an 8″ quiche (Serves 6 as a starter.):

For the Pastry

- 250g Plain Flour
- 125g Unsalted Butter, **cold & cubed**
- Pinch of Salt
- 1 Egg
- 1 tbsp Cold Water
- 1 Egg white, **beaten for glaze**

For the Filling

- 2 Large Onions
- 1 tbsp (15g) Butter
- 90ml Milk
- 90ml Double Cream
- 2 Eggs
- 1 tbsp Fresh Rosemary, **chopped**
- 50g Gruyere Cheese, **grated**
- Salt & Pepper

Essential Equipment

- 8" Round, Fluted, Loose Bottomed Tin
- Food Processor

To make the pastry, put the flour, butter & salt into a food processor & blitz until it becomes like fine breadcrumbs.

Beat the egg with the water & gradually pour into the food processor while it's still on. Stop when the pastry starts to clump together. Tip out onto your work surface & bring together to form a ball. Cover in clingfilm, flatten into a disc and rest in the fridge for 30 minutes.

Between two sheets of cling film, roll out your pastry into a rough circle approx 2 - 3 mm thick and big enough to cover the base & sides of your tin. Peel off one layer of cling film, and using the other to help, lift the pastry over your tin (cling film on top) and press into the edges.

KITCHEN
Mason

Press round the top of the tin edge to cut away the excess pastry then peel off the cling film and prick the base all over with a fork. Place into the freezer to chill for 30 minutes before baking.

Preheat your oven to 190°C/Fan 170°C and place a baking tray large enough to fit your tin on, into the centre.

Peel and slice the onions as finely as you can and melt the butter in a large, non stick frying pan over a low heat.
Add in the onions & cook, stirring often so they don't catch on the bottom, for about 30 minutes. They should be golden and soft. Leave to one side to cool.

Scrunch up a large piece of baking paper, (*not* greaseproof as that will stick) place over the pastry and cover with baking beans or rice. Place into the preheated oven on the hot baking tray and bake for 20 minutes.

Take out the oven and remove the baking paper & beans.

Brush all over with beaten egg & place straight back into the oven for another 10-12 minutes until a light golden brown. Leave to cool.

In a jug, beat together the milk, double cream, eggs, chopped rosemary & a very generous amount of salt and pepper to season.
Lay the caramelised onions over the base and spread out evenly.

Pour over the egg mixture until it reaches the top of the pastry case.

You may wish to do this after placing the tin in the oven to avoid any spillages.

Lastly, sprinkle all over with the gruyere cheese and, with the oven still at 190°C/Fan 170°C, bake for 25-30 minutes until the cheese on top is bubbling and golden.

Allow to cool for 5 mins in the tin then remove, slice and serve with a small salad.

Cheese Puffs with Fiery Tomato Salsa

This starter requires a little bit of effort but it's *totally* worth it! These puffs are a savoury, cheesy profiterole teamed up with a fiery salsa. A great, fun way to start any meal! Here is what you will need to serve 6 – 8.

For the Tomato Salsa

- 2 tbsp Olive Oil
- 1 Small Onion, **finely chopped**
- 1 Garlic Clove, **crushed**
- Splash of White Wine
- 400g Tin of Chopped Tomatoes
- 1 tbsp Tomato Purée
- ¼ - ½ tsp Chilli Flakes *(Depending how hot you like it)*
- Dash of Tabasco Sauce
- Pinch of Sugar
- Salt & Pepper

For the Cheese Puffs

- 70g Plain Flour, **sifted**
- 50ml Olive Oil
- 150ml Water
- 2 Eggs, **beaten**
- 55g Parmesan, **grated**
- ½ tsp Smoked Paprika
- Salt & Pepper
- Oil for Deep Frying

Essential Equipment

- Deep Fat Fryer (Or large pan & a thermometer)

To make the salsa, heat the olive oil in a large non stick frying pan. Add the onion and fry until softened but not browned. Next add the garlic, cook for a further 30 seconds then add the wine. Allow to bubble for 10-20 seconds then add the remaining ingredients to the pan. Mix well and simmer for 10-15 minutes until nice and thick. Season with salt & pepper to taste and pour into a serving bowl.

To make the cheese puffs, place the olive oil and water in a large saucepan. Bring to a rolling boil then throw in the flour and vigorously beat with a wooden spoon until a lump of dough forms. Tip the dough into a glass bowl and set aside to cool for a few minutes.

Now, with a truck load of elbow grease, gradually beat the eggs into the dough. It will feel like the mixture is splitting each time but stick with it & it should come together.

You are aiming for a 'dropping' consistency. (When you pick the mixture up with a spoon it will drop back to the bowl within 5 seconds.)

Once all the eggs are used up, add in the parmesan cheese & the paprika. Season well with salt & pepper and give it a final mix.

Fill a deep fat fryer with oil and heat to approx 180/190°C. Alternatively, fill a large saucepan with oil and heat until it reaches the same temperature.
When the oil is hot enough, carefully drop in teaspoon sized balls of the mixture. Fry for 2-3 minutes until golden. They should puff up and float to the surface.

Allow to drain on kitchen paper for a minute or two and repeat until all the mixture is used up. Serve the cheese puffs warm alongside the fiery salsa dip.

Chorizo Scallops

Ok, I know it's not exactly a cheap starter, but what's it all for if you can't splash out on the good things in life every now and then?? This indulgent recipe is a fantastic way to start any dinner party and I guarantee it will have your guests asking for seconds! Perfect served alongside a simple green salad or some crusty sourdough bread. Here is what you will need to serve 4 with a small salad.

- 80g Chorizo Sausage, **sliced**
- 300g Small Scallops
- Salt
- 3 tbsp Freshly Squeezed Lemon Juice
- 3 tbsp Fresh Parsley, **chopped**

Heat a large non stick frying pan over a medium heat and add in the slices of chorizo.
Fry until they have released lots of flavourful oils and are nice & crispy.

Remove the chorizo from the pan and turn the heat up to high.
Lightly season the scallops with salt then place into the hot pan. Cook on each side for about 1 – 2 minutes. Scallops can quickly be overcooked, especially small ones. However, you do want a nice golden colour to them so keep a watchful eye on the pan.

When the scallops are cooked, return the chorizo back to the pan and add the lemon juice.
Let it bubble vigorously for 1 minute.

Divide between 4 plates. Pour over any juices left in the pan, sprinkle with the chopped parsley & serve.

KITCHEN

"Eggs & Cheese"

This is a very light starter. Perfect if you have a heavy main course and/or dessert planned. It's also naturally vegetarian and gluten free so great if you have anyone with allergies coming to dinner! Here is what you will need to serve 6.

- 6 x Eggs
- 3tbsp Parmesan, **grated**
- 2 tbsp Mayonnaise
- 2 tbsp Fresh Chives, **finely chopped**
- 1 Fresh Red Chilli, **deseeded & finely chopped**
- Salt & Pepper, **to taste**
- Little Gem Lettuce Leaves, **to serve (optional)**
- 12 x Full length Chive Strands, **to serve (optional)**

Put the eggs in a pan and cover with cold water. Place over a high heat, bring to the boil then reduce to a simmer and cook for a further 7 minutes. Plunge into a bowl of ice cold water (to prevent the yolks from going green) and allow to cool.

Once they're cold, peel the shells and cut the eggs into halves.
Remove the yolks and rub them through a sieve and into a large bowl.

Add all the remaining ingredients and mix well.

Spoon the mixture back into the halved egg yolk holes.

Present on lettuce leaves topped with a single chive. Cover and chill until ready to serve.

Garlic & Thyme Baked Camembert

If Heaven really exists, it's filled with melted camembert! I usually just slice a cross in the top and bake but this gorgeous recipe takes it up a level. Adding hints of garlic & thyme, that silky melty cheese becomes the stuff of dreams… Here is what you will need to serve 3-4

- 1 x 250g Wheel of Camembert
- 1 Garlic Clove
- Sprig of Thyme
- Garlic Infused Olive Oil
- Your Choice of Bread, to serve*

*I used a granary baguette

Preheat your oven to 180°C/Fan 170°C.

Remove the camembert from it's plastic wrapper & place either back in its wooden box, or into a fitted dish. Slice a cross hatch pattern in the top of the cheese. Try not to cut into the sides.

Roughly slice the garlic clove then wedge them into the lines you've just cut.

Tear the leaves off a sprig of thyme and scatter them over the top. Press a few into the cuts to really get the flavour in. Drizzle a little garlic olive oil over the top then place it onto a baking tray.

Bake in the centre of the preheated oven for 20 minutes then allow to stand for 5 minutes to cool & set slightly before serving.

Ham & Cheese Pinwheels

This recipe is deceptively simple. Ok so we cheat a little by using shop bought dough, but you can still take all the credit because they look so good! A fantastic starter encompassing the much loved ham and cheese combo. You can't go far wrong really! Here is what you will need to serve 4.

- 400g Pack of Ready Rolled Pizza Dough
- 200g Grated Mozzarella
- 220g Smoked Ham
- Olive Oil for greasing
- Sweet Chilli Sauce, **to serve**

Preheat your oven to 200°C/Fan 190°C and grease a large baking tray with a little oil.

Remove the pizza dough from its outer packaging but leave it on the greaseproof sheet it's rolled in. (This will help you later.)
Top the dough evenly with the ham leaving a half inch (1.5cm) border all the way around the edge.

Scatter evenly with the grated mozzarella cheese.

Now for the fun bit. Using the greaseproof paper to help, roll the dough up as tightly as you can making sure to tuck in any stray bits of filling.

When you get to the edge, pinch the seam together really well, all the way along to make sure you won't have any leaks.
Pinch together both ends to seal everything in, then place seam side down onto the prepared tray.
Brush all over with a little olive oil then bake for 35 - 40 minutes until cooked and a lovely golden brown.

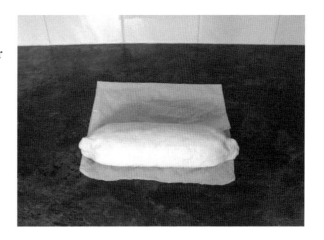

Allow to cool for 10 minutes before slicing into 8 pieces with a serrated knife.
Serve 2 slices per person with a dip of your choosing. I like mine with sweet chilli.

Healthy Pitta "Pizzas"

Ok, so this is pretty much the dream starter. It only takes 10 minutes to prepare, it's super cheap to make & it still tastes really good! Honestly, I'm not making it up! Here is what you will need to serve 4. (Would also make a nice light lunch.)

- 4 Pitta Breads
- 2 Tomatoes, **thinly sliced**
- 1 Ball of Fresh Mozzarella, **roughly torn**
- 35g of Fresh Rocket
- Garlic Infused Olive Oil
- Salt & Pepper

Heat the grill and toast the pitta breads for about 2-3 minutes on each side, until they are lightly golden and crispy. Lay some tomato slices over the top of each one and season with a little salt.

Top them all with a handful of rocket & some torn mozzarella pieces.

Drizzle generously with the garlic infused olive oil and a little salt & pepper to taste.
Serve immediately.

Posh Cheese & Onion Tarts

I'm all for making everything from scratch if you can, but it just seems impossible with our busy lifestyles now! Meet me in the middle and give these impressive Posh Cheese & Onion Tarts a try at your next dinner party. Ok, so we cheat a little and use ready made pastry, but the topping more than makes up for it! Here is what you will need to serve 6:

- 2 Red Onions
- 2 Yellow Onions
- 2 tbsp Honey
- 1 tbsp Olive Oil
- ½ Star Anise
- 2 Sprigs of Thyme + Extra for Decoration
- Salt & Pepper
- 2 tbsp Red Wine
- 1 x 375g Pack of Ready Rolled Puff Pastry
- 1 Egg + 1 tbsp Water
- 1 x 100g Ball Mozzarella

Peel & quarter the onions.
Heat a large non stick frying pan over a medium heat then add in the honey, olive oil & star anise. Allow to come to the boil then add the quartered onions & the 2 sprigs of thyme. Fry for about 2 minutes.

Add 30ml of water to the pan and a generous helping of salt & pepper. Give it a good stir, bring it to the boil and allow to simmer for 10 minutes.

Turn the heat up to high and pour in the red wine. Allow to bubble away for a minute then break the onions apart with a wooden spatula or spoon.

Reduce the heat again and simmer for a further 10 minutes until the onions start to become soft. Remove from the pan and allow to cool completely before using.

Preheat the oven to 200°C/Fan 190°C and line a large baking tray with baking paper or a silicone baking mat. You may need two trays.
Divide the pastry into 6 squares. (About 13 x 13cm) Beat the egg together with 1 tbsp of water and brush all over the pastry.
Prick the pastry all over with a fork, leaving a 1.5cm border around the edges. Transfer the squares to the prepared baking trays.

KITCHEN

Divide the onion mixture between each pastry over the pricked middle, being careful to still leave that 1.5cm border. Shred the mozzarella and scatter over each tart. Sprinkle with a little fresh thyme and top with some salt & pepper.

Bake in the preheated oven for 15 – 20 minutes until golden & risen. Allow to cool for a couple of minutes before transferring to serving plates.

Sweet Potato & Cumin Soup

Soup is a traditional starter but who says the flavour has to be?! This beautiful sweet potato & cumin soup is just the right balance of sweet and spice, a perfect way to start any dinner party! Here is what you will need to serve 6. (Makes approx 2.25 litres)

- 40g Unsalted Butter
- 2 Onions, **diced**
- 2 Garlic Cloves, **crushed**
- 1kg Sweet Potatoes, **peeled & chopped**
- 2 Celery Sticks, **chopped**
- 1 Green Apple, **peeled cored & chopped**
- 1 ½ tsp Cumin
- 2 litres Chicken Stock
- Natural Yoghurt & Croutons, **to serve (Optional)**

Essential Equipment

- Very Large Pan / Pot
- Stick Blender or Food Processor

Place the pan over a low heat and add the butter. When it's melted, add in the onion and cook for about 10 minutes until soft & translucent.

Add in the garlic, sweet potato, celery, apple &
cumin. Cook for a further 5 minutes until
everything is nicely coated.

Add the chicken stock and turn up the heat to high
to bring it all to a boil. When boiling, reduce the
heat and continue to simmer for about 30 minutes
until the vegetables are all soft.

Allow to cool before blending or you could burn
yourself. (Let's be honest, we've all made an
accidental mess with a blender before!)
Blend in the pan with a stick blender or in batches
in a food processor until smooth.

KITCHEN

To serve straight away, return the soup to a clean pan and warm through. Give it a quick taste and add as much salt & pepper as you think it needs.

Divide between serving bowls, add a dollop of natural yoghurt & a few croutons if you like.

Alternatively, you can pour into bags and freeze for later use. Defrost thoroughly before reheating.

Tomato & Rocket Salad

Who says that making a starter has to be difficult? The last thing you want is to be stressed out before hosting a dinner party! Try this simple but beautiful tomato & rocket salad. Not only does it taste great, it looks great too! I'll be honest, there's not many salads that actually appeal to me but this is one I will make again & again. It's also easy on the purse strings too. Win! Here is what you will need to serve 3 - 4

- 500g Charlotte Potatoes
- Salt & Pepper
- Good Glug of Italian Salad Dressing *
- 125g Cherry Tomatoes
- ½ Small Red Onion
- 35g Bag of Fresh Rocket
- Parmesan Shavings, **to serve**

You could make your own, but why pay for 10 ingredients when you can get a readymade one cheaper??

Cut the potatoes into equal sized pieces. (About 1".) I like to leave the skin on but you can peel it off if you want to.

Place in a medium saucepan & cover with cold, salted water. Bring to the boil then simmer for about 8-10 minutes until just soft but still firm enough to hold their shape.

Drain the potatoes and place in a large bowl. Stir through the Italian salad dressing while they're still hot, so they absorb all those lovely flavours. Leave to one side to cool.

Meanwhile, quarter the cherry tomatoes & thinly slice the red onion.

When the potatoes are cool, mix in the tomatoes, red onion, half the rocket and season with salt & pepper.

Transfer to a serving dish and top with the remaining rocket & some parmesan shavings. Serve immediately.

If you want to make this ahead, don't add the rocket until right before serving or it will wilt.

Mains

Chicken Teriyaki

Cod Curry

Creamy Pesto Chicken

Juicy Chargrilled Lime Chicken

Korean Beef

One Pot Creamy Garlic Pasta

One Pot Pizza Pasta

Slow Cooker BBQ Chicken

Spicy Sausage Pasta

Tasty Turkey Meatballs

Tomato & Mascarpone Risotto

Mains

Chicken Teriyaki

This traditional Japanese recipe is seriously delicious! The sweetness from the Mirin teamed up with the saltiness from the soy creates a stunning sauce that works so well with the chicken and the rice. Give this a go and I promise you will have your guests begging you for the recipe! Here is what you will need to serve 2 (easily doubled).

For the Chicken

- 50ml Light Soy Sauce
- 50ml Mirin
- 2 tbsp Caster Sugar
- 2 Chicken Breasts, **skinless & boneless**
- Salt & Pepper
- 1 tbsp Rice Bran Oil

For the Rice

- 1 x Garlic Clove, **crushed**
- 4 x Spring Onions, **chopped**
- 2 – 3 Small Mushrooms, **chopped**
- 250g of Cooked & Cooled Rice (or Microwave Rice)
- Salt & Pepper
- Pinch of Chilli Flakes **(optional)**

Essential Equipment

- Large Ovenproof Saucepan
- Large Non Stick Frying Pan

Preheat your oven to 200°C/Fan 180°C.

Put the soy sauce, mirin & caster sugar into the ovenproof saucepan. Bring to the boil then reduce the heat and simmer for about 15 mins until it becomes a sticky syrup.

Meanwhile, season both sides of the chicken breasts with a little salt & pepper. Heat a large non stick frying pan over a medium/high heat then add the oil. Fry the chicken breasts for about 5 minutes on each side, until they're a nice golden colour.

Place the part cooked chicken into the syrup & spoon the sauce over to coat. Put into the preheated oven for about 15-20 minutes until the chicken is cooked through. Turn the chicken over halfway through the cooking time and spoon the sauce over again.

Meanwhile, using the pan you fried the chicken in, fry the garlic and mushrooms for 1-2 minutes over a medium heat. Add a little more oil if you need to.

Add the spring onions and cook for a further 2 minutes.

Add in the rice, season with salt & pepper to taste and the chilli flakes if using. Keep warm over a low heat, stirring occasionally, until the chicken is ready.

When the chicken is cooked, remove from the saucepan and cut into slices.

Spoon the rice into serving bowls and lay the chicken on top. Pour over any leftover sauce and devour immediately!

Cod Curry

It's no secret that I'm not a huge lover of fish, but I'm finding that the more I try it, the more I'm starting to enjoy it. A curry is a great way to introduce fish to the fussy eater in your life and cod is a relatively inoffensive fish, so is far more likely to appeal to people like me! Fussy eaters aside, this curry has bags of flavour and the addition of chickpeas makes it satisfyingly filling too. Don't forget to leave room for pudding though! Here is what you will need to serve 4.

- 2 Large Tomatoes
- 1 tbsp Sunflower or Vegetable Oil
- 1 Small Onion, **diced**
- 1 Garlic Clove, **minced**
- 1" piece of Fresh Ginger, **minced**
- 150ml Fish Stock
- 1 tbsp Balti Curry Paste
- 1 tsp Ground Coriander
- 400g Tin of Chickpeas, **drained**
- 500g Cod Fillet, **cut into large chunks**
- 2 – 3 tbsp Fresh Coriander, **chopped**
- 3 – 4 tbsp Natural Yoghurt
- Salt & Pepper

Serve with boiled rice

Essential Equipment

- Blender (I used a Mini Blender)

Peel the tomatoes. I find it easiest to quarter them, then hold one end whilst sliding the knife underneath to remove the skin.

Heat a large, non-stick frying pan over a low heat. Add in the oil. Fry the onions, garlic and ginger for about 5 minutes until soft.

Transfer the mixture to a mini blender along with the chopped, peeled tomatoes and blitz until smooth.

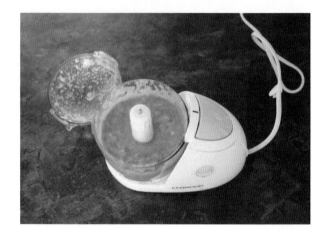

Return it to the pan then add the fish stock, curry paste, ground coriander & chickpeas. Mix well then simmer over a low heat for 10 – 15 minutes until thickened.

If it becomes too thick, just add a little more fish stock or water to loosen it again. Give it a taste, add salt & pepper if you think it needs it.

Season the cod with a little salt then add to the pan.

Stir gently to cover in the sauce, then simmer for another 5 minutes until the fish is cooked through. Don't stir too much though or the fish will fall apart.

Take off the heat and leave to rest for a few
minutes before stirring through the coriander &
yoghurt.

Divide between 4 plates & serve with cooked
basmati rice.

Creamy Pesto Chicken

We don't always have time for elaborate & intricate recipes. Sometimes we just want simple, great tasting food that doesn't take 10 hours to make! This fantastic one pot chicken dish is not only good for you, it creates minimal pot washing and it's absolutely bloomin' delicious! I'd say that's a winner, winner chicken dinner wouldn't you? Here is what you will need to serve 2. (Easily doubled.)

- 2 Chicken Breasts, **skinless and boneless**
- Salt & Pepper
- 1 tbsp Olive Oil
- 150g Cherry Tomatoes, **halved**
- 3 tbsp Pesto
- 3 tbsp Crème Fraîche
- Fresh Basil, **optional**

In-between cling film or in a freezer bag, flatten out the thickest part of the chicken breasts with a rolling pin. This will even them out and make cooking a little quicker & easier. Season both sides of each breast with salt.

Heat a large non-stick frying pan over a medium heat then drizzle in the oil. Add the chicken breasts and fry one side until nicely golden. (About 5-10 minutes.) Turn the chicken over & continue to cook for a further 12-15 minutes, until golden and cooked through. (You can cut through the middle of one to check if you need to.)

Add the halved cherry tomatoes to the pan and cook until starting to soften. (About 5 minutes.)

Turn down the heat and add in the pesto & crème fraîche. Season generously with salt & pepper then give it a good stir. Warm through for a couple of minutes before taking off the heat.

Divide between two plates, scatter with some torn basil leaves and serve with rice or potatoes.

Juicy Chargrilled Lime Chicken

This Chargrilled Lime Chicken is the juiciest chicken I have ever eaten in my life! It's so easy to make too. Simply dump the chicken in a bag with all the marinade ingredients, leave to marinate then grill. That's literally it. Moist, tasty, incredible chicken. I highly recommend allowing 24-48 hours to let the flavours really develop. Here is what you will need to serve 3. (Easily doubled)

- 30ml Light Soy Sauce
- 30ml Balsamic Vinegar
- 1 tbsp Olive Oil
- 1 tbsp Brown Sugar
- 2 tsp Worcestershire Sauce
- 2 tsp Honey Mustard
- 2 tsp Dried Thyme
- 2 Garlic Cloves, **crushed**
- Juice of 1 Small Lime
- 3 Chicken Breasts
- Cooked Rice or Couscous, **to serve**
- Chopped Parsley, **to serve (optional)**

Essential Equipment

- Large Zip Lock/Freezer Bag
- Griddle Pan

Add all the ingredients for the marinade into the large zip lock bag and give it a good mix. I find it easiest to open the bag out in a bowl and fold the top over to keep it steady.

Add the chicken to the bag, seal the bag then give it all a damn good mush around.

Leave to marinate in the fridge for 24-48 hours. At the *very* least, 3 hours.

Take the bag out the fridge when you're ready to cook. Then, using a rolling pin, carefully bang the thickest parts of the chicken to flatten a little. This makes cooking easier and more even. Do be tactful though or you'll pop the bag like I did & have to clean up raw chicken marinade juice from everywhere!

Heat a griddle pan over a medium heat. When the pan is hot, add your chicken.

Want the pretty charred lines? Don't touch them! Leave them exactly where they are for 5-8 minutes (depending on the size of your chicken breasts).

Once the timer beeps, flip them over and repeat for another 5-8 minutes.

As soon as they're cooked through, wrap them in a bit of tin foil and allow to rest for 5-10 minutes. This will help all those lovely juices stay *inside* the meat instead of pouring out.

Serve alongside some rice, couscous or even a salad. Enjoy!

Korean Beef

I'm always looking for new ways to cook minced beef. The regular 'fry it and chuck a jar of sauce over it' gets a little boring! This Korean recipe is sincerely yummy. It's *insanely* quick to make too! Perfect to knock up if you have impromptu guests to cater for. Here is what you will need to serve 2 - 3 (Easily doubled.)

- 1 tbsp Sesame Oil
- 3 Cloves of Garlic, **minced**
- 500g Lean Minced Beef
- 70g Dark Muscovado Sugar
- 60ml Light Soy Sauce
- ½ tsp Fresh Ginger, **minced**
- ½ tsp Chilli Flakes
- Salt & Pepper
- Bunch of Spring Onions, **sliced**

Serve with boiled rice.

Place a large non stick frying pan over a medium heat.
When the pan is hot, add in the oil to warm through for a few seconds then add the garlic. Fry for 30 - 40 seconds then add in the minced beef. Add in a generous helping of salt & pepper then continue to cook until the mince is brown and cooked through. Break up the mince with a wooden spoon/spatula as it cooks.

When the mince is browned, add the sugar, soy sauce, ginger & chili flakes into the pan. Stir through and cook for a few minutes just to allow the flavours to blend together.

Have a taste, add some more salt & pepper if you think it needs it.

Serve over boiled rice and top with a generous sprinkling of sliced spring onions.

One Pot Creamy Garlic Pasta

I *love* pasta and I *love* garlic! Making this One Pot Creamy Garlic Pasta a big hit in the Kitchen Mason household! It's quick, made in just one pan & seriously satisfying. So that's fast food, with minimal pot washing & big flavour. Well I don't know about you but I'm sold! Here is what you will need to serve 2. (Easily Doubled.)

- 1 tbsp Olive Oil
- 2 Garlic Cloves
- 250ml Chicken Stock *
- 300 - 500ml Semi Skimmed Milk
- 1 tbsp Unsalted Butter
- 150g Dried Linguine Pasta
- Salt & Pepper
- 15g Parmesan, **grated**
- 1 tbsp Parsley, **finely chopped**

* *For a vegetarian version, use vegetable stock.*

Essential Equipment

- Large non stick Frying Pan (Big enough to fit the pasta)**

****Don't have a pan big enough? Snap the pasta so it fits!*

Place the frying pan over a medium heat and add the olive oil. Swill around the pan a little then add in the garlic. Cook for about 1 minute stirring frequently so it doesn't burn, until you can really smell it.

Next, add in the chicken stock, 300ml of milk and the butter. Season with a little salt & pepper and stir until the butter is melted.

Add the pasta to the pan and bring to the boil. Reduce the heat and allow to simmer, stirring occasionally, for about 15 - 20 minutes. Until the pasta is cooked or 'al dente' for you posh folk.

If the sauce gets a little thick during cooking, you may want to add more milk to the pan. Use your judgement.

When the pasta is cooked, stir through the grated parmesan & the parsley. Have a taste, add more salt & pepper if you think it needs it and add a little more milk if you want to loosen the sauce.

Give it all a good stir & divide between 2 warmed bowls. Serve immediately.

One Pot Pizza Pasta

Isn't it beautiful?? This sensational One Pot Pizza Pasta recipe really does taste like pizza! Genuinely one of the most delicious pasta dishes I have ever created in the Kitchen Mason kitchen. Even the Mr wholeheartedly agrees! I won't keep you waiting any longer than I have to, let's get straight to it. Here is what you will need to serve 4.

- 4 Pork Sausages
- 1/2 Onion, **finely diced**
- 1 Garlic Clove, **finely diced**
- 1 x 500g Jar of Bolognese Sauce
- 1 tsp Dried Basil
- 1 tsp Dried Oregano
- Salt & Pepper
- 150g Dried Fusilli Pasta
- 100g Mozzarella Cheese, **grated**
- 30g Parmesan Cheese, **grated**
- approx 12 Slice of Pepperoni

Essential Equipment

- Large Oven Proof Lidded Frying Pan

Firstly prep your ingredients. Squeeze out the sausage meat from their casings, finely dice the onion & garlic and grate the cheeses.

Heat the frying pan over a medium/high heat then add the sausage meat, onion & garlic. Break apart the sausage meat with a wooden spatula and continue to cook until the meat is no longer pink & the onion is translucent.

Add the bolognese sauce then fill the empty jar up with water and add that too. Stir through the basil oregano and a generous helping of salt & pepper.

Bring to the boil then add in the dried pasta. Reduce the heat to medium, cover with a lid and simmer for 10-15 minutes until the pasta is cooked to your liking. Meanwhile, preheat your grill.

When the pasta is cooked, give it a good stir then top with the grated cheeses and the pepperoni.

Place under the grill for a few minutes until the cheese is melted then divide between 4 plates/bowls and tuck in!

Slow Cooker BBQ Chicken

Having a busy lifestyle doesn't mean you have to miss out on incredible food. Turns out, it's super easy with a slow cooker! One of the most forgotten about kitchen appliances that really can churn out some amazing meals. This shredded BBQ chicken recipe is no exception! It requires next to no effort, very little 'hands on' time & minimal pot washing. Yet still manages to deliver flavour in a big way. Go on, let the slow cooker do all the hard work for you! Here is what you will need to serve... lots!

- 900g (4 Large) Chicken Breasts, **skinless & boneless**
- Salt & Pepper
- 250ml BBQ Sauce
- 60ml Italian Salad Dressing
- 50g Light Brown Sugar
- 1 tbsp Worcester Sauce

Essential Equipment

- Slow Cooker (Mine has 3.5 litre capacity.)

Place the chicken breasts into the slow cooker & season both sides of each one with salt & pepper.

In a medium sized bowl, mix together the BBQ sauce, Italian salad dressing, brown sugar & Worcestershire sauce until smooth. Pour the sauce into the slow cooker and mix until the chicken is completely covered.

Pop the lid on and cook on high for 3 - 3 and a half hours, until the chicken is cooked through. Take one breast out at a time & shred in a bowl using the backs of two forks together (or beat in an electric stand mixer briefly for a quicker result).

When it's all nicely shredded, dump it back into the slow cooker for 10 - 15 minutes on warm to soak up all those lovely BBQ juices!

Serve in toasted bread rolls, with chips, over boiled rice or with pasta.

Spicy Sausage Pasta

In need of a quick, easy and tasty midweek meal idea? Look no further! This super speedy dish is packed full of flavour and really simple to make. I've even served this at a dinner party and received nothing but yummy noises and thumbs up all round! Here is what you will need to serve 2. (Easily doubled.)

- 200g Conchiglie Pasta*
- 1 tbsp Olive Oil
- 4 Hot & Spicy Sausages
- 90ml Dry White Wine
- 90ml Double Cream
- 1 heaped tsp Honey Mustard
- Pinch of Chilli Flakes
- ½ bunch Fresh Basil, **roughly chopped**

* Any shape pasta will do. (Fusilli, penne etc) I like conchiglie as it traps all the pieces of sausage.

Get a large pan of generously salted water to the boil and cook the pasta according to packet instructions.

Meanwhile, heat a large, heavy based saucepan over a medium heat. Add in the oil then squeeze the sausage meat out of their cases and into the hot pan.

Using a wooden spatula, break up the meat and fry until nicely browning. (About 5 minutes.)

Then pour in the wine and simmer for a minute or two until the sausages have *almost* absorbed it. (About 2 minutes.)

Now pour in the double cream, mustard, chilli flakes (if using) and season well with salt & pepper. Give it a good stir and heat through for a minute or two.

When the pasta is cooked, drain and add it to the pan **along with a little of the pasta water**. This starchy liquid will help to emulsify the sauce - meaning, it will bring it all together and help it to stick to the pasta as opposed to making a pool of liquid at the bottom of your bowl. Win.

Add in the basil and give it all a good stir. Serve in warmed bowls and devour!

Tasty Turkey Meatballs

There is something so homely and comforting about meatballs. I don't know what it is but it's always such a satisfying meal! This marvelous recipe is no exception. But hang on a minute... it's *healthy*? Shut the front door! Yes seriously. Made with lean turkey mince & tinned tomatoes, these Turkey Meatballs not only look the part, they *taste* the part AND they're good for you! Here is what you will need to serve 4.

Turkey Meatballs (Makes 28-30)

- 500g Turkey Mince
- 2 tsp Garlic Powder
- 2 tsp Ground Cumin
- 2 tsp Ground Coriander
- 2 tsp Onion Salt *

For the Sauce

- 2 x 400g Tins of Chopped Tomatoes with Herbs
- Salt & Pepper
- Pinch of Sugar
- 3 – 4 tbsp Parmesan Cheese, **grated**

For the Couscous

- 250g Couscous
- 300ml Chicken Stock
- 2 – 3 tbsp Coriander, **chopped**

Alternatively you can use 2 tsp onion powder & ¼ tsp of salt.

In a large bowl, mix together the turkey mince & all the spices with a fork.

Scoop out heaped teaspoon sized balls of the mixture and roll into balls. If you have the time, place them on a baking tray lined with foil, cover with cling film & leave overnight to allow the flavours to develop.

Preheat your oven to 210°C/Fan 200°C. Place the meatballs into the bottom of a large, oven proof dish and bake for 20 minutes.

Mix the tinned tomatoes with the sugar and season with salt & pepper. Pour the tomatoes over the meatballs and give it a little stir. Sprinkle the top with the parmesan cheese & place back into the oven for another 20 minutes.

Meanwhile, make the couscous.

Weigh out the couscous in a large bowl then pour over hot chicken stock. Stir quickly with a fork, cover with cling film & leave to one side until just before the meatballs are ready. Then fluff up the couscous with a fork & stir through the chopped coriander

Divide the couscous between 4 bowls & top with the meatballs.

Tomato & Mascarpone Risotto

People seem to think that risottos are complicated to make when, in actual fact, all it requires is a bit of patience and a little multi tasking. If you add the stock gradually, you can't go far wrong! They make very impressive dinner party mains too. Here is what you will need to serve 2 (or 4 as a Starter).

- 500ml Chicken Stock *
- 50g Unsalted Butter
- 250g Cherry Tomatoes, **halved**
- 2 – 3 tbsp Garlic Infused Olive Oil
- 200g Arborio Rice
- 100g Mascarpone Cheese
- 25g Parmesan Cheese, **grated**
- Salt & Pepper
- Handful of Rocket Leaves**, to serve (optional)**

Use vegetable stock to make the dish vegetarian. I use stock pots but any type of stock is fine.

Essential Equipment

- Large non stick Frying Pan
- 2 x Saucepans
- Sieve

Make up your chicken/vegetable stock and keep at a gentle simmer in one of the saucepans.

In the other saucepan, melt the butter over a medium heat and add the halved tomatoes. Cook, stirring occasionally, whilst we get on with the rice.

Heat the frying pan over a medium heat then add the oil. Tip the rice in and stir to coat all the grains in the oil.

Now, a ladleful at a time, add the stock into the rice. Stir constantly and make sure that all the liquid has been absorbed before adding the next ladleful. It will take about 15 - 20 minutes.

Meanwhile, the tomatoes should be nice and soft after about 10 minutes cooking.

Tip them into a sieve set over a small bowl and push through with a spoon. This will remove the skins & the seeds.

Once the rice is cooked (it should still have a little bit of bite to it) add in the tomato mixture, the mascarpone & the parmesan. Have a taste and season with salt & pepper.

Go easy on the salt though as the parmesan is already very salty.

Risotto is best served immediately so divide it between 2 bowls if you are using it for a main or 4 bowls if you are having it as a starter.
Top with a handful of rocket leaves & a little more parmesan if you like.

Desserts & Sweet Treats

Butterscotch Tart

Choc Chip Cookie Bars

Chocolate Oreo Tart

Easy Caramel Pecan Fudge

Easy One Bowl Brownies

Gooey Lemon Pudding

Mango & White Chocolate Cheesecake

Microwave Maltesers Fudge

Nutella Stuffed Peanut Butter Cookies

Raspberry Crumble Bars

Salted Caramel Choux Buns

Victoria Sandwich Cake

Butterscotch Tart

I absolutely *adored* this pudding when I was in school. Before I left, I even went as far as to ask a dinner lady for the recipe! It was on this scrappy little bit of paper that got mislaid over the years. I honestly thought it was lost forever until one day, I was being nosy at my parents house (as you do) and to my surprise, found the scrappy bit of paper with the recipe on it! It was a little vague but I happily filled in the gaps. Here is what you will need to serve 6 - 8.

For the Pastry

- 250g Plain Flour
- 125g Unsalted Butter, **cold & cubed**
- Good pinch of Salt
- 1 Egg, **beaten**
- 1 Egg, **beaten for glaze**
- Cold Water

For the Filling

- 175g Unsalted Butter
- 175g Golden Caster Sugar
- 175g Plain Flour
- Pinch of Salt
- 1 tsp Vanilla Extract
- 1 tsp Butterscotch Essence/Flavouring
- 110ml Semi Skimmed Milk

Essential Equipment

- 20cm (8") Round Loose Bottomed Fluted Tin

To make the pastry, put the flour, cubed butter & salt into a food processor & blitz briefly until it resembles fine crumbs. (If you don't have a food processor, put the ingredients into a large bowl and rub between fingers & thumbs until the same result is achieved.)

Then add <u>one</u> of the beaten eggs and a **little** cold water. Blitz again briefly until it just starts to come together to form a dough. (Or mix together with your hands.)

Tip the dough out and gently/briefly bring together into a ball. Place into some clingfilm, flatten into a disc and refrigerate for 30 minutes.

KITCHEN
Mason

Preheat your oven to 190°C/Fan 170°C.
Once the dough is chilled, place between two pieces of clingfilm and roll out a circle to a thickness of about 2-3mm.

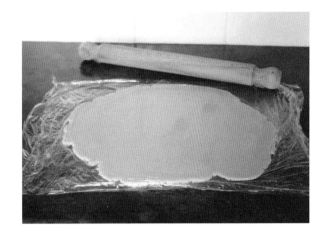

Peel off one layer of cling film, and using the other to help, lift the pastry over your tin (cling film on top) and press into the edges.

Press round the top edge of the tin to cut away the excess pastry.

Peel off the cling film and prick the base all over with a fork. Loosely cover with cling film and pop into the freezer for 10 minutes. This should stop the butter from melting too quickly and, therefore, the sides from shrinking too much.

Scrunch up a large sheet of baking paper (NOT greaseproof paper as that will stick) and place into the pastry case. Fill with baking beans or rice and bake in the preheated oven for 15mins.

Remove from the oven, take out the beans & baking paper. Brush the pastry all over with the 2nd beaten egg and pop back into the oven for a further 10-12 minutes until golden brown. Allow to cool completely before adding the filling.

To make the filling, in a very large saucepan, melt the butter and the sugar together over a low heat. Stir until the sugar has dissolved.

Add in the flour and cook, beating vigorously with a wooden spoon, for 2-3 minutes. You just need to 'cook out' the flour so it doesn't taste chalky.
If the mixture starts to split & butter seeps out, don't panic! We'll solve that later.

Tip the mixture into a large mixing bowl and add in the salt, vanilla, butterscotch & milk. Beat until smooth and thick. To start with, it will feel like it just won't come together, but keep going, it will. If your mixture split & you're having a hard time bringing it together, pop it all into a food processor and blitz on high until smooth and thick. It will be fine I promise.

When the pastry case is completely cooled, pour the filling in and allow to set at room temperature for at least 30 minutes to an hour. It should be able to just hold it's shape when cut.

Choc Chip Cookie Bars

Who doesn't love a good choc chip cookie?! So why not turn them into Choc Chip Cookie Bars? I know! I think it's a great idea too, I'm glad we agree. These Choc Chip Cookie Bars are really easy to make & perfect when you're expecting company, to take into the office or even for your next bake sale. Here is what you will need to make 16 small or 9 large.

- 115g Unsalted Butter, **soft***
- 200g Light Brown Sugar
- 1 Egg
- 1 tsp Vanilla Extract
- 125g Plain Flour
- 1/2 tsp Salt
- Pinch of Bicarbonate of Soda
- 150g Milk Chocolate Chips

*If your butter isn't really **really** soft, melt it instead.*

Essential Equipment

- 23cm (9″) Square Baking Tin/Dish

Preheat your oven to 180°C/Fan 170°C and grease & line the base and 2 sides of the baking tin/dish.

In an electric stand mixer or a large bowl with an electric hand whisk, beat together the butter (really soft or melted) and the sugar until very light and fluffy.

Add in the egg & the vanilla and beat again until smooth. Scrape the bowl down half way through.

Sift in the flour, salt & bicarbonate of soda. Fold in using a spatula. Don't overdo it, just fold until you can't see anymore flour.

Stir through **two thirds** of the chocolate chips.

Tip the mixture into the prepared tin/dish and press evenly, right into the corners. Top with the remaining chocolate chips and bake in the preheated oven for 20-25 minutes.

It should be golden and a little crunchy on top when done.

Allow to cool completely in the tin/dish before removing and slicing into 9 or 16 bars. Store in an airtight container at room temperature and consume within 4-5 days.

Chocolate Oreo Tart

This decadent, silky chocolate beauty is much easier to make than it looks. Perfect for the chocolate lovers in your life it's bound to have people asking for seconds! Plus, any no bake pudding is a winner in my book. Here is what you will need to serve 8 – 10.

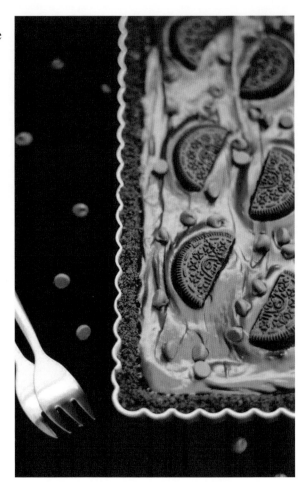

For the Base

- 300g Oreos
- 100g Unsalted Butter

For the Filling

- 200g Dark Chocolate
- 55g Unsalted Butter
- 190ml Double Cream

For the Decoration

- 4 Oreos (Taken from the 300g already listed)
- Handful of Chocolate Chips

Essential Equipment

- 10 x 35cm (4 x 14") Fluted Loose Bottomed Rectangular Tart Tin
- Food Processor

Reserving 4 biscuits for decoration, tip the rest of the Oreos into a food processor, fillings and all, and pulse until fine crumbs are formed.

Gently melt the butter in a small saucepan (or in the microwave) then pour over the the Oreos in the processor. Pulse a few times until it starts to clump together.

KITCHEN

Tip the mixture into the tart tin & press firmly into the base and sides with a metal spoon.
Pop it into the freezer to firm up whilst we get on with the filling.

Finely chop the dark chocolate & cube the butter. Place it all into a large glass bowl and set to one side.

Pour the cream into a small saucepan and gently heat until it *just* comes to the boil.

Pour over the chocolate and leave to stand for 5 minutes. Then give the mixture a good stir with a wooden spoon. It should become a bowl of silky smooth chocolate heaven!

Pour the mixture straight over the prepared base and smooth out with either a spoon or spatula.

Cut the reserved Oreos in half and press into the top. Scatter over some chocolate chips to finish and place into the fridge to set for at least an hour before serving. (The ganache filling should become firm enough to slice.)

Easy Caramel Pecan Fudge

Caramel Pecan Fudge, I guarantee it tastes just as good as it looks! Did I mention that it's ridiculously easy to make too? It literally takes minutes in the microwave then the fridge does all the hard work for you. Here is what you will need to make 36 devilishly delicious pieces.

- 525g White Chocolate
- 1 x 397g Can Condensed Milk
- 55g Unsalted Butter, **cubed**
- 1/2 tsp Vanilla Extract
- 125g Pecans, **roughly chopped**
- 50 - 100g Caramel Sauce

Essential Equipment

- 20 x 20cm (8 x 8") Square Baking Pan or Silicone Pan
- Piping Bag
- Skewer or Cocktail Stick

Lightly grease and line the base & sides of the baking pan. If you are using a silicone one like me, you don't need to line it.

Break the chocolate into a large microwavable bowl then add the condensed milk & the butter. Melt in the microwave on full power for 30 seconds. Give it a good stir then heat again in 10 to 20 second intervals stirring well between each time until it's smooth & melted.

Add in the vanilla extract and the chopped pecans and stir until mixed well.

Working quickly so the fudge doesn't begin to set, pour the mixture into the prepared tin and smooth out with a spatula.

Load the caramel into a piping bag & snip a small bit off the end. Pipe thin-ish lines along the fudge.

Take a skewer/cocktail stick or even a sharp knife & gently drag lines up then down along the whole thing. Pop into the fridge to set completely for a good 4 hours or overnight. When it's firm, remove from the pan and slice into 36 pieces. (A 6 x 6 grid.)

Store in an airtight container in the fridge for up to 1 week. (Not that it will last that long!)

Easy One Bowl Brownies

This Amazing Easy One Bowl Brownies recipe is so ridiculously simple to make and yields *incredible* results! Fudgy, chewy, rich chocolate brownies made with half the effort in half the time. Seriously, you'd be out of your mind not to try this one! Here is what you need to make 9 large or 16 smaller bars.

- 110g Unsalted Butter
- 110g Dark Chocolate
- 2 Eggs
- 225g Golden Caster Sugar
- 1 tsp Vanilla Extract
- 1/4 tsp Salt
- 60g Plain Flour
- 2 tbsp Cocoa Powder

Essential Equipment

- 20cm (8″) Square Baking Tin
- Large Microwavable Bowl

Grease & line your baking tin with baking paper then preheat your oven to 180°C/Fan 170°C.

Add the butter into a large bowl and break in the chocolate. Melt in the microwave in 20 second intervals, stirring well between each time. Try not to overheat. Leave to one side for a few minutes to cool to room temperature.

One at a time, beat in the eggs. Mix very well.

Add in the sugar and give it a really good beating with a spatula or whisk. It should stop being really grainy and become quite smooth.

Stir through the vanilla & salt then sift in the flour & cocoa powder.

Fold it all together with a spatula but don't overdo it. Fold just until you can't see anymore flour left in the batter.

Pour the lot into your prepared tin and smooth out evenly.

Bake in the oven for 20-25 minutes. It will likely be a little crispy on top but fear not, there is lots of gorgeous chocolatey goo underneath!

Allow to cool completely before removing from the tin and slicing into 9 or 16 bars. Store in an airtight container (I prefer metal) at room temperature and consume within 5 days.

Gooey Lemon Pudding

This pudding is just perfect for those cold winter nights when you want to cosy up next to the fire and dream of sunshine. It would be wonderful served on it's own, drizzled with a little cream, dusted with icing sugar or even with some warm custard. Go on, give your Winter evenings a burst of Summer! Here is what you will need to serve 6 – 8

- 60g Unsalted Butter, **room temp**
- 300g Golden Caster Sugar
- 2 Lemons (Zest of both, Juice of 1)
- 3 Eggs, **separated & room temp**
- 240ml Single Cream, **room temp**
- 50g Plain Flour

Essential Equipment

- 20cm (8") Square Baking Dish
- A larger pan that fits the Square Baking Dish within, **for cooking**

Preheat your oven to 180°C/Fan 170°C & grease a 20cm (8") square baking dish with butter.

Either in a stand mixer or in a large bowl with an electric hand whisk, beat together the butter, sugar & zest of both lemons until very light and fluffy. At least 5 minutes.

One at a time, add in the egg yolks. Beating well in-between each addition. Then in thirds, alternately add the cream & the flour to the mixture. Don't overmix, only beat until the ingredients are *just* blended.

Either in a stand mixer or in a large bowl with an electric hand whisk, whip the egg whites until glossy and stiff. (Make sure the bowl is clean. Any fat will stop the egg whites from gaining volume.)

In quarters, gently fold the lemon mixture into the egg whites. Be very careful not to knock the air out of the whites.

When the ingredients are nicely blended together, pour into the buttered baking dish. (Pour close to the dish or you could burst the air bubbles in the egg whites.)

Set the dish into the larger pan and place into the preheated oven. Pour just boiled water to halfway up the square dish then close the oven door and bake for 45 minutes until the top is nice and golden.

This dessert is best served straight from the oven and should be cake like on top but beautifully gooey at the bottom.

KITCHEN
Mason

Mango & White Chocolate Cheesecake

This stunning cheesecake is so light and refreshing! It's great if you've eaten quite a heavy meal, perfect for a Summer pud or just fancy something fruity. A slightly surprising combination, mango and white chocolate actually work very well together! Here is what you will need to serve 8.

- 150g Digestive Biscuits
- 50g Unsalted Butter
- 425g Tin of Mango Slices
- Zest & Juice of 1 x Lime
- 300g White Chocolate
- 280g Philadelphia Original Cream Cheese*
- 150ml Double Cream

*Don't substitute the cream cheese for a lighter version as the cheesecake won't set.

Essential Equipment
- 20cm (8") Round Springform Pan
- Food Processor

Lightly grease and line the base of your tin, set to one side until needed.

Roughly break the biscuits into a food processor and pulse until fine crumbs. Melt the butter in a saucepan over a low heat or in the microwave. Pour it into the biscuit crumbs then pulse until it starts to clump together. Tip the mixture into the prepared tin and press firmly. Place into the fridge whilst we make the filling.

Drain the mangoes and place the slices into a food processor along with the zest & juice of the lime. Blitz until you get a nice smooth purée.

Break the chocolate into a large bowl. Gently melt either in 20 second intervals in the microwave, stirring well between each blast, or set over a pan of barely simmering water.

In another bowl, lightly whip the double cream until soft peaks form.

In a large bowl, whisk the Philadelphia cream cheese until soft & smooth.

Carefully fold in the melted white chocolate and the whipped cream until it's all blended together.

Pour in two thirds of the mango purée and stir together. Then pour the mixture over the biscuit base.

Dot the remaining mango purée on the surface and, using a skewer or a knife, swirl it around to create a marbled pattern.

Place in the fridge to set for a minimum of 3 hours, preferably overnight, before removing from the tin, slicing and serving.

Microwave Maltesers Fudge

This Microwave Maltesers Fudge requires just 3 ingredients to make & 5 minutes of your time. Seriously, I'm not kidding! It really is incredibly delicious too. Super creamy fudge crammed *full* of crunchy Maltesers. Little bites of actual heaven. How much more convincing do you need? Here is what you will need to make 36 large bite size pieces.

- 400g Milk Chocolate
- 1 x 397g Tin of Condensed Milk
- 400g Maltesers

Essential Equipment

- 20cm (8″) Square Baking Tin or Silicone Pan
- Large Microwavable Bowl

Line your baking tin and set to one side. If you're using a silicone pan you don't need to line it.

Break the chocolate into a large microwavable bowl and pour in the condensed milk. Heat in the microwave for 30 seconds then give it a good stir. Repeat, heating in 10 second intervals until it's all melted and smooth.

Working quickly, tip in all bar about 15-20
Maltesers and give it a mix. (It will start to set
very swiftly!)

Tip the whole lot into your prepared/silicone tin
and level out with a spatula.

Take those 15-20 Maltesers you reserved earlier
and press them randomly into the top.
Pop into the fridge to set for at least 4 hours or
overnight. Once firm, remove from the tin & slice
into 36 pieces (a 6 x 6 grid).

Store in an airtight container in the fridge and consume within 5 days. In my opinion it is best eaten on the day you cut it but only because when air gets to the inside of a Malteser, it goes a bit sticky & gooey. Any whole Maltesers that are within the fudge will remain very crunchy though. Which more than makes up for any stickiness!

Nutella Stuffed Peanut Butter Cookies

This recipe is nowhere near as fiddly or complicated as you might think. With a simple bit of advanced preparation, you'll be enjoying these surprisingly delightful treats in no time! Here is what you will need to make 20 – 25 cookies.

- 250g Nutella
- 220g Plain Flour
- 1 tsp Bicarbonate of Soda
- ¼ tsp Baking Powder
- ¼ tsp Salt
- 180g Unsalted Butter, **room temp**
- 100g Golden Caster Sugar
- 90g Soft Light Brown Sugar
- 190g Smooth Peanut Butter
- 1 Large Egg, **beaten**
- ½ tsp Vanilla Extract

Line a baking sheet with baking paper. Then spoon out 25x teaspoon sized blobs of Nutella onto it and pop into the freezer for at least an hour until solid. (Overnight is fine if you want to plan ahead.)

Preheat your oven to 180°C/Fan 170°C and line a large baking tray with a silicone baking mat or baking paper.

Sift together the flour, bicarbonate of soda, baking powder & salt and set to one side.

In an electric stand mixer or a large bowl with an electric hand whisk, beat together the butter & sugars until light and fluffy

Add in the peanut butter and beat again until nice & smooth.

Add in the egg, vanilla extract and mix until smooth again.

In thirds, add in the flour mixture and beat until no more flour is visible.

Take the Nutella blobs out the freezer. Spoon out 2 tbsp of the cookie dough and flatten slightly in your palm. Place a Nutella blob in the middle and wrap the dough around it. Make sure the Nutella is completely covered to avoid any leakages. Place spaced apart on the prepared baking sheet.

Press them down a little then take a fork and criss cross the prongs gently into the top to make a pattern.
Repeat until the baking tray is filled (but not over crowded.) You will need to cook in batches so pop the Nutella blobs back into the freezer in-between each batch.

Bake in the preheated oven for 12 minutes, turning half way to ensure an even bake.

Leave to cool on the tray for a few minutes until firm enough to transfer to a wire rack to cool completely. Rinse and repeat until you have used up all the dough. These will keep for 3-4 days in an airtight container at room temperature. (Not that they will last that long!)

Raspberry Crumble Bars

These delightful little creatures are the perfect afternoon tea accompaniment! They're so simple to make and seriously yummy. You can quite easily change up the flavour too, just swap the jam to a different one. Strawberry, apricot, whatever takes your fancy! Here is what you will need to make 9 bars.

- 130g Plain Flour
- ¼ tsp Bicarbonate of Soda
- ¼ tsp Salt
- 85g Rolled Oats
- 110g Light Soft Brown Sugar
- 115g Unsalted Butter, **room temp**
- 245g Raspberry Jam

Essential Equipment

- 8" (20cm) Square Baking Tin

Preheat your oven to 180°C/Fan 170°C and line the base & 2 sides of the square tin. Leave a slight overhang to make it easier to remove later.

In a large bowl, mix together the plain flour, bicarbonate of soda, salt, oats & sugar.

Cube the butter and add into the oats. Using your thumbs and forefingers, rub the butter into the oats to create a crumble mixture. Don't overmix, just rub until the ingredients are evenly blended.

Press half the mixture into the base of the prepared tin.
Leaving a half inch (1.5cm) border around the edges, evenly spread the jam on top of the oats.

Scatter the remaining crumble mixture on top to completely encase the jam within the oats. Press down a little.

Bake in the preheated oven for 35 – 40 minutes until golden brown. If your oven has hot spots, turn the tin halfway through for a more even bake.

Allow to cool completely in the tin before removing and cutting into a 3 x 3 grid making 9 bars.
These are best kept in a metal container at room temperature. They will keep for 4 – 5 days.

Salted Caramel Choux Buns

Choux pastry is another thing that has a reputation of being difficult to make. If you follow this recipe, I promise you good results! You just need a good amount of elbow grease and a little patience. Not convinced? This sumptuous salted caramel flavour will tempt you into giving it a go I'm sure of it! Here is what you will need to make 14 buns.

For the Portion of Salted Caramel
- 75g Unsalted Butter
- 50g Soft Light Brown Sugar
- 50g Golden Caster Sugar
- 100g Golden Syrup
- 125ml Double Cream
- Approx 2 tsp Sea Salt

For the Choux Pastry
- 220ml Water
- 80g Unsalted Butter
- Pinch of Salt
- Generous pinch of Sugar
- 125g Plain Flour
- 220g Beaten Egg (approx 4 Eggs) **room temp***

For the Filling
- 750ml Double Cream
- 1 Portion of Salted Caramel **(Ingredients above)**

For the Caramel Icing
- 60g Unsalted Butter
- 110g Soft Light Brown Sugar
- 2 tbsp Milk
- 120g Icing Sugar

For the Drizzle
- 75g Dark Chocolate
- 1 – 2 tbsp Milk

I do recommend weighing the eggs. Eggs can vary in size but weight is absolute and will guarantee a good outcome.

Place a large glass bowl into the fridge to chill ready for the choux pastry later.

To make the salted caramel, place the butter, both sugars and golden syrup in a small saucepan over a medium heat and melt together. Bring it to the boil and allow to simmer for 3 minutes. (Swirl once or twice if you need to.)

Turn down the heat, add in the cream and give it a good stir. Now, half a teaspoon at a time, add the salt, stirring well and tasting in-between each addition. (**WARNING** - be <u>very</u> careful not to burn yourself as it will still be hot!)

When it's right for you, decant into a bowl, cover with cling film and pop into the fridge to chill until needed later.

Onto the choux pastry.

Lightly grease two large baking sheets (or line with silicone baking mats) and preheat your oven to 200°C/Fan 190°C.

In a medium sized saucepan, add the water, butter, salt & sugar. Heat until the butter has melted and it *just* comes to the boil.

With the pan still over the heat, dump in the flour and beat vigorously with a wooden spoon until it comes together to form one lump of dough.

Remove from the heat and tip the dough into that bowl you chilled in the fridge earlier. Leave to cool for 5 minutes.

When cooled, add the beaten egg to the dough a little at a time and beat vigorously with a wooden spoon in-between each addition. At first it will split and seem like it is never going to come together but it will, trust me. Keep going.

You're after a 'dropping consistency.' (When you lift up a large amount of the dough, it should drop back to the bowl within 5 seconds.)

Pour the pastry into a large piping bag fitted with a large round nozzle. Evenly spaced out, pipe 14 'blobs' about 5cm in diameter. Try and keep them all the same shape and size if you can but don't worry too much.

Gently dampen the tops with a little cold water. (If there are any 'spikes' of pastry, gently pat them down a little.)

Pop them straight into the oven and bake for 20 - 25 minutes.

Remove them from the oven and, using either a skewer or a sharp knife, poke an air hole into each one then place straight back into the oven for a further 10 minutes. This will help to dry out the inside and prevent them from collapsing.

When they are crispy & golden, remove from the oven and place onto a wire rack to cool completely.

Meanwhile, make the filling. You could use a stand mixer with the whisk attachment but I like to do this by hand as you can very easily over whip cream. So, using a large bowl and a whisk, whip the cream until soft peaks form.

Remove the salted caramel you made earlier from the fridge and fold into the cream in thirds until smooth & blended together.

I used a 'filling' nozzle which made life alot easier but if you don't have one, just use your judgement and pick the best from what you have. So, prepare your piping bag with your chosen nozzle, fill with the cream then squeeze in the filling. When they're all filled, leave to one side whilst we make the caramel icing.

In a small saucepan, melt together the butter, sugar & milk. Bring it to the boil then simmer for 2 minutes.

Remove from the heat and add in the icing sugar. Beat until smooth. If it starts to set before you've covered all your buns, just pop it back over the heat again to melt a little and stir well.

Spoon the warm icing over each bun then allow to set at room temperature. (This should happen relatively quickly.)

KITCHEN
Mason

Now if you want to make them look really tempting, make this quick chocolate drizzle. Simply break the dark chocolate into a large bowl and add in the milk. Then either in the microwave in 20 second intervals or over a pan of barely simmering water, gently melt until shiny and smooth.

Pour into a piping bag and snip the end. Pipe zig zags over each bun, stand back, and marvel at your beautiful creations...

Victoria Sandwich Cake

This back to basics Victoria Sandwich Cake is perfect for baking with your little ones. It's one of the first cakes I ever made and one I still enjoy making to this day! You can't go far wrong with vanilla sponge, jam & buttercream can you?! Here is what you will need to serve 8 – 10.

For the Sponge

- 200g Golden Caster Sugar
- 200g Unsalted Butter, **room temp**
- 4 Eggs, **room temp**
- 200g Self Raising Flour
- 1 tsp Baking Powder
- 2 tbsp Milk
- 1 tsp Vanilla Extract **(optional)**
- ¼ tsp Salt

For the Filling

- 100g Unsalted Butter, **room temp**
- 140g Icing Sugar
- ½ tsp Vanilla Extract
- Approx 300g Strawberry Jam
- Icing Sugar for Dusting

Essential Equipment

- 2 x 20cm (8") Round Loose Bottom Cake Tins

Lightly grease the base & sides of your cake tins & line the bases with baking paper. Preheat your oven to 190°C/Fan 170°C.

Either in an electric stand mixer or a large bowl with an electric hand whisk, add in all the sponge ingredients & mix together until smooth & lump free.

Divide the batter evenly between the two tins & smooth with a spatula. To prevent the cake from doming so much in the middle, put a 'dip' in the centre of the batter. Place in the centre of the preheated oven (preferably on the same shelf) for about 15-20 minutes or until a skewer inserted into the centre comes out clean.

Leave to cool in the tins for 10 minutes. Then slide a pallet knife around the sides of each cake to loosen, remove from the tin, peel off the baking paper from the base & leave to cool completely on a wire rack before decorating.

To make the buttercream filling, place the butter, icing sugar & vanilla extract into either an electric stand mixer or a large bowl with an electric hand whisk. Mix slowly to start with (or you may find yourself head first in a mushroom cloud of icing sugar!) then increase the speed and beat until light and fluffy. (At least 3-4 minutes.) Scrape down the sides of the bowl periodically and if you need to loosen the mixture a little, add a splash of milk and continue to mix.

Once the sponge layers have completely cooled, place one layer onto a cake stand. If you need to, level the top by slicing any domed cake off with a large, sharp knife. Then smear the buttercream evenly all over the top, right to the edges.

Top with the jam and spread out evenly. Not quite to the edges, but close. Remember this will squash outwards slightly when you put the top layer on.

When you're happy with that, top with the remaining sponge layer. I like to use the bottom side up to give a nice flat edge. But it's entirely up to you. Place a heaped teaspoon or two of icing sugar into a sieve, then generously sprinkle all over the top of the cake.

Store in an airtight container and eat within 2 days.

Seasonal

Red Velvet Cupcakes

Creme Egg Brownies

Blood Spatter Cookies

No Bake Bloody Spider Web Chocolate Tart

Pumpkin Pretzels

Bonfire Cupcakes

Christmas Pud Teacakes

Christmas Tree Brownies

White Chocolate & Cranberry Tiffin

Red Velvet Cupcakes

Here's a great Valentine's Day gift idea for you. Red Velvet Cupcakes. Is there anything *more* Valentines than red velvet? With a gorgeously decadent cream cheese frosting, these are the perfect indulgence for you and your other half. Here is what you need to make 12.

For the Decorations *

- White Fondant Icing
- Red/Pink Fondant Icing
- Heart Shaped Cutters

* I recommend you make these 24hrs in advance if you can.

For the Cake

- 60g Unsalted Butter, **Room Temp**
- 150g Golden Caster Sugar
- 1 Egg, **Room Temp**
- 10g Cocoa Powder
- 2 tbsp Red Liquid Food Colouring **OR** 2 tsp Red Food Colouring Gel
- ½ tsp Vanilla Extract
- 120ml Buttermilk
- 150g Plain Flour
- ½ tsp Salt
- ½ tsp Bicarbonate of Soda
- 1 ½ tsp White Wine Vinegar

For the Cream Cheese Frosting

- 300g Icing Sugar
- 50g Unsalted Butter, **Room Temp**
- 125g Philadelphia Original Cream Cheese **

**Don't use a cheaper alternative or a 'lighter' version or your cream cheese frosting will end up potentially very runny/wet.

Essential Equipment

- 12 Hole Cupcake Tin
- 12 Foil Cupcake Cases

To make the decorations, on a work surface lightly dusted with icing sugar, roll out the red & white fondant to about 3mm thick & cut using heart shaped cutters of your choosing.

If you are sticking shapes together, just dab on a little cold water and press lightly together. They will stick when dried.

Once you've cut out your shapes, place them on a tray lined with baking paper at room temperature to dry for 24 hours. (You can speed up this process by placing them in the fridge.)

Onto the cake. Preheat your oven to 170°C/Fan 160°C & line a 12 hole cupcake tin with cases. (I prefer to use foil cases as they don't seep grease.)

Either in an electric stand mixer or a large bowl with an electric hand whisk, cream together the butter & sugar until light & fluffy.

Beat the egg and gradually add this into the bowl. Mix on a high speed until well incorporated and smooth.

In a little bowl, mix together the cocoa powder, food colouring & vanilla extract to make a paste. If you are using a gel colour you may need to add a little water to loosen it. You're looking for a deep red colour. (Remember that colours lighten once baked so don't be skimpy!)

Add the paste into the butter mixture and mix until smooth. Scrape down the sides of the bowl then mix again to ensure the colour is evenly distributed.

With the stand mixer/electric hand whisk on a slow speed – gradually add in **half** the buttermilk and mix until smooth. Then sift in **half** the flour and mix again until smooth. Repeat until all the buttermilk & flour are used up. Then add in the salt, bicarbonate of soda & white wine vinegar and mix on a medium/high speed until smooth.

Divide evenly between the 12 cupcake cases. (They should be about half to two thirds full.)

Bake in the preheated oven for 18-25 minutes. To test, insert a skewer into the middle of a cupcake. If it comes out clean, they're cooked. If there is batter on it, they need a little longer.

Once cooked, allow to sit in the tin for a couple of minutes then transfer to a wire rack to cool completely before decorating.

Meanwhile, let's get on with the cream cheese frosting.

Sift the icing sugar into the bowl of an electric stand mixer and add the butter. Mix on a medium/slow speed until well mixed. (Or use an electric hand whisk & a large bowl.)

Add in the cream cheese & mix slowly to start with (until the icing sugar is no longer a risk of mushroom clouding your kitchen!) then mix on high until really light and smooth for about 5 minutes.

Be careful not to over do it though, cream cheese frosting is a delicate creature & will become very runny if you over mix it.

Chill in the fridge until ready to decorate your cupcakes.

When you're cakes are completely cool, load a large piping bag with a nozzle of your choosing & fill with the cream cheese frosting.

I used a 3M open star nozzle and piped frosting from the outside edge inwards.

Then simply top with your sugar heart decorations and et vous voila!

I usually say not to put cake in the fridge as it will dry it out quicker. However, due to the cream cheese frosting, I recommend it with this particular recipe.

They should keep for 3-4 days in a cardboard cupcake box. (If possible, don't store in plastic as the sugar decorations will sweat.)

Creme Egg Brownies

So how about we kick things up a notch for Easter with these awesome Creme Egg Brownies?! They look amazing, they *taste* amazing & I bet everyone asks you for the recipe... Definitely better than an Easter egg! Here is what you will need to make 9 generously sized brownies.

- 200g Unsalted Butter, **Room Temp**
- 250g Dark Chocolate (good quality)
- 100g Milk Chocolate (good quality)
- 3 Eggs, **Room Temp**
- 250g Dark Muscovado Sugar
- 1 tsp Vanilla Extract
- 50g Self Raising Flour
- 5 x Cadbury's Creme Eggs

Essential Equipment

- 20cm/8″ Square Baking Tin
- Electric Stand Mixer **or** Electric Hand Whisk

Preheat the oven to 190°C/Fan 170°C and grease & line the base and sides of the baking tin.

In a glass bowl set over a pan of barely simmering water, break in the dark & milk chocolate and add the butter. Gently melt, stirring occasionally. Then remove from the heat, stir until smooth & shiny and allow to cool whilst we move onto the eggs. Alternatively, you can do this in the microwave by heating on full power for 30 seconds. Stir well then heat in 10-20 second intervals stirring between until melted and smooth. Allow to cool.

Either in an electric stand mixer with the whisk attachment or using a large glass bowl & an electric hand whisk, crack in all 3 eggs and whisk for at least 3-4 minutes on a high setting. They should end up pale in colour and very light.

Add in the muscovado sugar & vanilla extract and whisk again until evenly blended but still fairly light in texture.

In thirds, pour the chocolate into the egg mixture and gently fold in using a spatula.

Once all the chocolate is incorporated, sift in the flour and fold until you can't see anymore flour.

Pour the mixture into the prepared tin and bake in the centre of the preheated oven for 20-25 minutes.

Meanwhile, cut the creme eggs in half. Heating the knife in hot water may help.

Take the brownie out the oven & place the halved
cream eggs onto it, bear in mind where you will
be slicing. Place back into the oven for a further
10 – 15 minutes. When done, there should still be
a little movement in the centre.

Allow to cool completely in the tin before
removing and slicing into 9 pieces. I know it's
hard, but trust me, be patient. It'll be totally worth
it!

Blood Spatter Cookies

These Blood Spatter Cookies look unbelievably awesome!! Not only that, they are ridiculously fun to make (particularly the spatter bit) and guaranteed to be a hit with guests and/or trick or treaters. You absolutely *have* to give them a go! Here is what you will need to make about 30 – 35 Cookies.

For the Cookies

- 250g Unsalted Butter, **Room Temp**
- 200g Golden Caster Sugar
- 1 tbsp Vanilla Extract
- 1 Egg, beaten
- 450g Plain Flour

For the Royal Icing

- 2 Large Egg Whites
- 500g Icing Sugar
- Squeeze of Lemon Juice
- Red Food Colouring Gel

Essential Equipment

- 7cm Cookie Cutter
- Piping Bag
- No.3 Writing Nozzle
- Piping Bottle*

You can use a piping bag fitted with a round nozzle but a bottle is a little bit easier.

BEFORE ATTEMPTING THIS RECIPE, PLEASE NOTE THE CHILLING & SETTING TIMES BETWEEN CERTAIN STAGES.

To make the cookies, either in an electric stand mixer or a large bowl with an electric hand whisk, cream together the butter, sugar & vanilla extract until light and fluffy.

Add the egg and beat again until it's all combined.

Tip in the flour and beat with a wooden spoon until it clumps together to form a dough.

Tip out onto a work surface and knead gently to bring together into a ball. Divide it into two, then roll each one in-between 2 large sheets of baking paper to 6mm/1/4″ thick. Place both into the fridge to chill for about an hour. This is important as if you don't chill the dough, when you cut out the cookies they won't hold their shape well.

To make the icing, in an electric stand mixer or a large bowl with an electric hand whisk, beat together the egg whites, icing sugar & lemon juice on high speed for about 5 minutes until stiff peaks form.

Adding <u>no more than a drop or two at a time</u>, **very** gradually add cold water and mix in-between each addition until it's thinned to soft peaks. Take 3-4 heaped tablespoons of the icing and place into a bowl. Immediately cover with cling film and set to one side. This will be used to pipe a border around each cookie to hold the icing in.

Back to the mixer. Once again, adding a <u>little at a time</u>, **very** gradually add cold water and mix in-between each addition until the mixture becomes a flooding consistency. Take 5–6 tablespoons of the icing and place into a small bowl. Colour with red food colouring gel then immediately cover with cling film. Set to one side. Pour the remaining icing into another bowl, immediately cover with cling film & set to one side with the others.

Once the dough is chilled, remove from the fridge and cut as many 7cm circles out as you can. Re-roll the leftover dough to the same thickness & cut more cookies until all the dough is used up. Chill the cookies for 15 minutes whilst you preheat the oven to 190°C/Fan 180°C.

Line a large baking sheet with baking paper or a silicone mat. Fill with cookie discs, leaving room between each one for possible spreading, then bake for 10 minutes until the edges are turning golden.

Allow the cookies to cool for a minute or two on the tray before transferring to a wire rack to cool completely. You will likely need to bake in batches so repeat the process for the remaining cookies.

On to the decoration! Once the cookies have completely cooled, load a piping bag with the writing nozzle. Give the border (soft peak) icing a good mix then spoon into the piping bag. Carefully pipe round the edges of each cookie and leave to set for 15 – 20 minutes.

When the borders have set hard, give the white flooding icing a good mix then pour into the piping bottle. Flood the centres of each cookie and leave to set for at least 1 – 2 hours.

Tic toc tic toc…

When the icing has *finally* set, we're ready for the really fun bit!

It's probably a wise idea to tape newspaper up the back of where you will be 'spattering' and also to place underneath the biscuits you are decorating.

I opted to decorate 3 – 4 at a time (mainly because I wanted to enjoy this bit for as long as possible!) but you could just as easily decorate all of them at once. It's entirely up to you.

Give the red flooding icing a good mix. Take a fork, dip it in the icing and go nuts. Fling that fork around like you're conducting Flight of the Bumblebee!

Leave the icing to set for another 1 – 2 hours then marvel at your incredible work…

Store in an airtight container and consume within 4-5 days.

No Bake Bloody Spider Web Chocolate Tart

How about this disgustingly delicious Chocolate Oreo Tart disguised as a gruesome & bloody spider web treat eh?! This no bake delight is terrifyingly tasty, easy to make & will blow your Halloween party guests' minds when they cut into it and reveal a bloody surprise. Here is what you will need to serve 8 – 10.

The Base

- 245g Oreos
- 80g Unsalted Butter

The Filling

- <u>Half</u> a 395g Tin of Caramel
- Red Food Colouring Gel
- 175g Dark Chocolate, **Finely Chopped**
- 50g Unsalted Butter, **Room Temp**
- 165ml Double Cream

To Decorate

- 50g White Chocolate
- Plastic Spiders, **Optional**

Essential Equipment

- 20cm (8″) Loose Bottomed Tart Tin
- Food Processor
- 1 x Disposable Piping bag

To make the base, tip the Oreos into the food processor (including the cream filling) and pulse until fine crumbs are formed. Then gently melt the butter in a small saucepan or in the microwave and pour into the processor with the Oreo crumbs. Pulse a few times until it starts to clump together.

Tip the mixture into the tin and press firmly into the base & sides with a metal spoon. Pop into the freezer to firm up whilst we crack on with the filling.

Pour the caramel into a bowl & add a generous amount of red food colouring gel using a cocktail stick. Mix really well. You can keep adding more colour until you reach your desired shade but make sure to do it a little at a time as you can always add more but you can't take it out!

Pour the 'blood caramel' over the chilled Oreo base & spread out evenly. Pop back into the freezer whilst we make the chocolate tart filling.

If you haven't already, finely chop the dark chocolate & cut the butter into small pieces. Place it all into a large glass bowl and set to one side.

Then pour the double cream into a small saucepan and gently bring to the boil. (Don't continue to let it boil – turn the heat off as soon as it *starts* to boil.)
Pour over the chocolate/butter and leave to stand for 5 minutes.

When the 5 minutes are up, give it a really good stir with a spatula. It should turn into a beautifully smooth & silky bowl of chocolate ganache heaven.

Pour the chocolate ganache over the 'blood caramel' and smooth out with a spatula. Working quickly, (as the ganache will start to set pretty fast) break the white chocolate into a bowl and microwave in 10 second intervals. Stir well between each time and keep heating until it's melted and smooth.

Pour the melted chocolate into the disposable piping bag and snip a small bit off the end. Starting from the middle of the tart working outwards, pipe a spiral of white chocolate.

Then using a skewer or knife, gently pull lines from the middle to the edge going all the way round the tart. It should end up looking like a spider's web.

And that's it! Pop it into the fridge to set for at least an hour before serving. Consume within 3-4 days.

Pumpkin Pretzels

This very simple recipe for pumpkin pretzels is perfect for getting the kids involved at Halloween. There's no sharp knives and no oven – just some melting & decorating! All the fun without any of the boring stuff. Plus, the whole salty/sweet thing is amazing! Here is what you will need.

- Large bag of M&M's
- 200-300g White Chocolate
- Orange Food Colouring Gel
- Bag of Salted Pretzels

Line a large baking sheet with baking paper or a silicone baking mat and remove all the green M&M's from the bag. (The bonus of only needing the green ones is you get to eat all the others later!)

Break the white chocolate into pieces and place into a large glass bowl. Microwave for 30 seconds then give it a stir. Continue to microwave in 20 second intervals, stirring between each time, until the chocolate is completely melted & smooth. Using cocktail sticks, add small amounts of the orange food colouring gel at a time until you get the colour you like. Make sure to stir well so all the colour is mixed in.

Now all you need to do is dip each pretzel into the orange chocolate and shake off the excess.

Place onto the prepared baking sheet & press a green M&M into the top. If the chocolate starts to get a little thick, pop it into the microwave for 10 seconds and give it a stir.

Place them into the fridge to set then store in an airtight container in the fridge for up to a week.

Bonfire Cupcakes

Celebrate Guy Fawkes Night in style with these eye catching Bonfire Cupcakes! Made with easy two tone frosting, Matchmakers & Cadbury's Flake, I guarantee they will bring fireworks to your party table! Here is what you will need to make approx 16.

For the Cake

- 80g Unsalted Butter, **Room Temp**
- 280g Golden Caster Sugar
- 200g Plain Flour
- 40g Cocoa Powder
- 1 tbsp Baking Powder
- ¼ tsp Salt
- 240ml Whole Milk, **Room Temp**
- 2 Eggs, **Room Temp**

For the Frosting

- 400g Icing Sugar, **Sifted**
- 200g Unsalted Butter, **Room Temp**
- 1 tsp Vanilla Extract
- Splash of Milk
- Orange Food Colouring Gel
- Yellow Food Colouring Gel

For the Decoration

- 1 x 130g Box of Matchmakers (I used Honeycomb flavour)
- 4 x Full Sized Cadbury's Flake Bars

Essential Equipment

- 2 x 12 Hole Cupcake Tins
- 16 Foil Cupcake Cases
- Piping Bag
- Large Star Nozzle

Line your cupcake tins with the foil cases and set to one side. Preheat your oven to 180°C/Fan 170°C.

In an electric stand mixer or a large bowl with an electric hand whisk, beat together the butter, sugar, flour, cocoa powder, baking powder & salt until it becomes like fine breadcrumbs.

In a jug, beat together the milk & the eggs. Pour two thirds into the dry ingredients and mix until really smooth. Add the remaining third and mix again until all the ingredients are blended well and smooth.

Fill each case to about 2 thirds full then bake in the preheated oven for 15 – 20 minutes until a skewer inserted into the middle comes out clean.

Transfer the cakes to a wire rack to cool completely whilst we make the frosting.

In an electric stand mixer or a large bowl with an electric hand whisk, beat together the butter, icing sugar & vanilla extract. Start slow (or you will be engulfed in a mushroom cloud of icing sugar!) then work up to a high speed. Beat on high for a good few minutes until the mixture is really light and smooth. Add a splash of milk to loosen it a little and mix again until smooth.

Divide the frosting between two bowls. Using cocktail sticks, add orange food colouring to one and yellow to the other. Keep gradually adding colour until you get the shades that you want.

Load a piping bag with a large star nozzle. Then carefully spoon one colour of frosting down one side of the bag and the other colour down the other side. It doesn't have to be exact, just roughly.

Have a little practice swirl on a plate to make sure that both colours are coming through, then pipe swirls on each cake by piping circles from the outside in. You may like to pipe another smaller swirl on top like I did. I think it looks good to have a tall fire under the "logs."

Snap some Matchmakers in half and others into smaller pieces. Cut the Flakes into small pieces. Start with a 'teepee' frame of 3 or 4 larger Matchmakers then dot smaller Matchmakers & pieces of flake around the bottom. Repeat until all the cakes are covered and look like super cute mini bonfires! Store in a cardboard cupcake box at room temperature & consume within 3-4 days.

Christmas Pud Teacakes

This one is great fun to make! Perfect for the little ones to get involved with too. Yes it might be cheating a little buying your own teacakes but just look how cute they are! No one will ever know... Here is what you will need to make 6, easy doubled, tripled or however many take your fancy!

- 1 x pack of 6 Chocolate Teacakes
- 60g Icing Sugar
- Green Fondant Icing
- Red Sugar Balls (or Red Fondant Icing)
- Edible Glue (or Water if using Red Icing)

Essential Equipment

- Small Holly Plunge Cutter

On a surface lightly dusted with icing sugar, roll out the green icing to about 3mm thick and cut out as many holly leaves as you need. (One per teacake.)

Stick 3 red sugar balls to the middle of each holly by painting on a little edible glue and pressing them on lightly. Alternatively, you can make little red balls from red icing (just tear off very small pieces & roll into balls between your fingers) and use a small dab of cold water to stick them into the centre of the holly. Place them onto a plate in the fridge to dry.

Meanwhile, to make the icing, simple weigh out the icing sugar into a small bowl and add 2 tsp of cold water. Give it a good stir until it's smooth and lump free. It should be quite thick but still a tiny bit runny.

Unwrap your teacakes and place them onto a tray or cooling rack.

'Splodge' about a tsp worth of icing onto the top and encourage a few dribbles down the sides. Yes splodge, that's a technical term.

Place a holly decoration onto the top of each one.

Leave to set for an hour (or overnight is fine) then store in an airtight container at room temperature. These will last for 1-2 weeks.

Christmas Tree Brownies

How cute are these Christmas tree brownies?! Not only are they delightfully gooey & rich, they're really fun to decorate AND vegetarian & gluten free. It's also a great recipe to get the kids involved in. What more could you want?! Here is what you will need to make 14.

One thing to note – these brownies work best if made the night before and allowed to cool **completely** before attempting to slice & decorate.

For the Brownie

- 250g Dark Chocolate **
- 100g Milk Chocolate **
- 200g Unsalted Butter, **Room Temp**
- Pinch of Salt
- 3 Eggs, **Room Temp**
- 250g Dark Muscovado Sugar
- 1 tsp Vanilla Extract
- 50g Gluten Free Self Raising Flour *

For the Decoration

- 100g White Chocolate **
- Pack of Candy Canes **
- Red/Green Sugar Balls **

Essential Equipment

- 30 x 20cm Rectangular Cake Tin

Regular self raising flour works fine if you don't need it to be gluten free.

** *Most are vegetarian/gluten free but check the label just in case.*

Grease and line the cake tin and set to one side until needed.
Preheat your oven to 190°C/Fan 170°C.

Break the dark & milk chocolate into a large bowl and add the butter & salt. Gently melt either in a bowl set over a pan of barely simmering water or in the microwave. Stir until smooth & shiny then leave to one side to cool.

Either in an electric stand mixer with the balloon whisk attachment or in a large bowl with an electric hand whisk – whisk the eggs for at least 3-4 minutes until really light and pale. It should leave a slight trail when you remove the balloon whisk/beaters.

Add in the muscovado sugar & vanilla extract and whisk again until evenly blended but still fairly light in texture.

In **thirds**, pour in the cooled chocolate & gently fold through using a rubber spatula. Sift over the flour and carefully fold this in – *just* until you can't see any more lumps of flour and the mixture is smooth & still quite light.

Pour the mixture into the prepared cake tin – be careful not to overfill as it will rise slightly.

Then bake in the preheated oven for approx 25-30 minutes.

As mentioned before, it is best to make these brownies the night before and allow to cool completely before attempting to remove from the tin & slice.

When completely cooled - run a spatula down the sides of the brownie to release from the tin then gently lift out and place on a chopping board/mat. Cut the brownie into 14 triangles. You will have 4 spare bits for you to taste test too. (See… one has gone already!)

Take each candy cane out the wrapper and snap into pieces approx 3cm long. Place the brownies on a wire rack over a piece of newspaper & carefully insert a piece of candy cane into the base of each one.

Melt the white chocolate in either a bowl set over a pan of barely simmering water or in the microwave and pour into a piping bag. Snip the end and pipe 'tinsel' across each tree then place sugar balls down the edges in the chocolate for the baubles. I found it best to decorate in half batches – just to ensure the chocolate doesn't set before you stick the 'baubles' in.

Allow the chocolate to set for about 30-40 minutes or so before either devouring or placing in nice presentation boxes to give as gifts to your loved ones.

I find it best to store these in an airtight container in the fridge – due to their extreme 'gooeyness' they can become a little delicate if stored at room temperature.

White Chocolate & Cranberry Tiffin

Kick off the start of Christmas advent with this incredibly delightful and suitably festive White Chocolate & Cranberry Tiffin. It's a little different to the rich, chocolate version I remember begging my Gran to make as a child, but my word – it's just as heavenly! Here is what you will need to make approx 24 pieces.

- 300g Digestive Biscuits
- 140g Unsalted Butter
- Pinch of Salt
- 3 tbsp Golden Syrup
- 1 tbsp Caster Sugar
- 2 tbsp Malted Milk Powder
- 140g Dried Cranberries
- 500g White Chocolate
- Red Food Colouring (**Optional**)

Essential Equipment

- 30 x 20 Rectangular Cake/Swiss Roll Tin

Lightly grease & line your cake tin and set to one side until needed.

Using either a food processor or a rolling pin and a plastic bag, blitz/bash the digestive biscuits until **almost** fine crumbs – but you want some chunky bits left in for added texture.

In a medium saucepan, gently heat the butter, salt, golden syrup, caster sugar & malted milk powder until the butter has melted and the sugar has dissolved.

Pour the liquid over the biscuit crumbs in a large bowl and mix until completely coated.

Throw in the cranberries and give it a good mix. (You may wish to chop them a little first if they are large cranberries as this will help the mixture bond together better with fewer 'gaps')

Press the mixture into the prepared tin then place into the fridge to harden/set for about 45mins to an hour. When the mixture has firmed up, we need to smother it in chocolate!

Break the white chocolate into a large bowl. Either in the microwave or set over barely simmering water, gently melt the chocolate until smooth and shiny.

Pour about 3 quarters of it over the tiffin. (Or all of it if you don't want to do the following decorative step.)

With the remaining quarter, add in some red food colouring & mix. Then pour into a piping bag and snip the end.

Work quickly as the chocolate will set and the 'feathering' technique won't work unless it is still melted.

Pipe stripes diagonally across the tiffin.

Then take a cocktail stick and draw lines through the chocolate. First stroke down, then the next – upwards. Repeat until you have 'feathered' the whole thing. Allow to chill in the fridge for about 45mins to an hour before slicing.

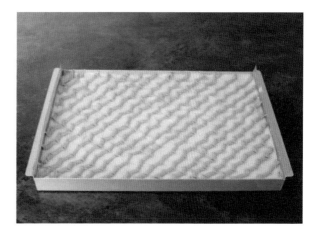

If you want evenly sized pieces, run a sharp knife under hot water before slicing each piece. This will melt through the chocolate preventing it from snapping into random shapes.

Store in an airtight container in the fridge and eat within 4 – 5 days.

Index

Candy Canes
Christmas Tree Brownies 147

Caramel
Easy Caramel Pecan Fudge 85
No Bake Bloody Spiderweb
Chocolate Tart 133
Salted Caramel Choux Buns 107

Celery
Sweet Potato & Cumin Soup 32

Cheese
Cajun Bean Dip with Cheesy Nachos 5
Caramelised Onion &
Rosemary Quiche 8
Cheese Puffs with Fiery
Tomato Salsa 13
"Eggs & Cheese" 19
Garlic & Thyme Baked Camembert 22
Ham & Cheese Pinwheels 24
Healthy Pitta "Pizzas" 27
Mango & White Chocolate
Cheesecake 94
One Pot Pizza Pasta 57
Posh Cheese & Onion Tarts 29
Tasty Turkey Meatballs 65
Tomato & Mascarpone Risotto 68

Cheesecake
Mango & White Chocolate
Cheesecake 94

Chicken
Chicken Teriyaki 39
Creamy Pesto Chicken 47
Juicy Chargrilled Lime Chicken 49
Slow Cooker BBQ Chicken 60

Chicken Stock
One Pot Creamy Garlic Pasta 54
Sweet Potato & Cumin Soup 32
Tasty Turkey Meatballs 65

Chickpeas
Cod Curry Page 43

Chilli
"Eggs & Cheese" 19

Chilli Flakes
Cheese Puffs with Fiery Tomato Salsa 13
Chicken Teriyaki 39
Korean Beef 52
Spicy Sausage Pasta 62

Chives
"Eggs & Cheese" 19

Chocolate
Choc Chip Cookie Bars 79
Chocolate Oreo Tart 82
Christmas Pud Teacakes 144
Christmas Tree Brownies 147
Creme Egg Brownies 123
Easy Caramel Pecan Fudge 85
Easy One Bowl Brownies 88
Mango & White Chocolate Cheesecake 94
Microwave Maltesers Fudge 97
No Bake Bloody Spiderweb
Chocolate Tart 133
Pumpkin Pretzels 138
Salted Caramel Choux Buns 107
White Chocolate & Cranberry Tiffin 152

Chocolate Chips
Choc Chip Cookie Bars 79
Chocolate Oreo Tart 82

Chocolate Teacakes
Christmas Pud Teacakes 144

Chorizo
Chorizo Scallops 17

Choux Pastry
Cheese Puffs with Fiery Tomato Salsa 13
Salted Caramel Choux Buns 107

Christmas Pud
Christmas Pud Teacakes 144

Cocoa Powder
Bonfire Cupcakes 140
Easy One Bowl Brownies 88
Red Velvet Cupcakes 119

Cod
Cod Curry 43

Conchiglie Pasta
Spicy Sausage Pasta 62

Condensed Milk
Easy Caramel Pecan Fudge 85
Microwave Maltesers Fudge 97

Cookies
Blood Spatter Cookies 127
Choc Chip Cookie Bars 79
Nutella Stuffed Peanut
Butter Cookies 100

Couscous
Juicy Chargrilled Lime Chicken 49
Tasty Turkey Meatballs 65

Coriander
Cajun Bean Dip & Cheesy Nachos 5
Cod Curry 43
Tasty Turkey Meatballs 65

Cranberries
White Chocolate &
Cranberry Tiffin 152

Cream
Caramelised Onion &
Rosemary Quiche 8
Chocolate Oreo Tart 82
Gooey Lemon Pudding 91

Cream Cheese
Mango & White Chocolate Cheesecake 94
Red Velvet Cupcakes 119

Cream Cheese Frosting
Red Velvet Cupcakes 119

Creme Eggs
Creme Egg Brownies 123

Crème Fraîche
Creamy Pesto Chicken 47

Croutons
Sweet Potato & Cumin Soup 32

Cumin
Sweet Potato & Cumin Soup 32
Tasty Turkey Meatballs 65

Cupcakes
Bonfire Cupcakes 140
Red Velvet Cupcakes 119

Curry
Cod Curry 43

Curry Paste
Cod Curry 43

D
Dark Chocolate
Creme Egg Brownies 123
Chocolate Oreo Tart 82
Christmas Tree Brownies 147
Easy One Bowl Brownies 88
No Bake Bloody Spiderweb
Chocolate Tart 133
Salted Caramel Choux Buns 107

Digestive Biscuits
Mango & White Chocolate Cheesecake 94
Red Velvet Cupcakes 119
Mango & White Chocolate
Cheesecake 94
No Bake Bloody Spiderweb
Chocolate Tart 133
White Chocolate & Cranberry Tiffin 152
Salted Caramel Choux Buns 107
Spicy Sausage Pasta 62

Double Cream
Caramelised Onion & Rosemary Quiche 8
Chocolate Oreo Tart 82
Mango & White Chocolate Cheesecake 94
No Bake Bloody Spiderweb
Chocolate Tart 133
Salted Caramel Choux Buns 107
Spicy Sausage Pasta 62

Dried Cranberries
White Chocolate & Cranberry Tiffin 152

E
Easy Caramel Pecan Fudge 85
Easy One Bowl Brownies 88
"Eggs & Cheese" 19

Edible Glue
Christmas Pud Teacakes 144

F
Fish
Chorizo Scallops 17
Cod Curry 43

Fish Stock
Cod Curry 43

Fondant Icing
Christmas Pud Teacakes 144
Red Velvet Cupcakes 119

Food Colouring Gel/Liquid
Bonfire Cupcakes 140
Pumpkin Pretzels 138
Red Velvet Cupcakes 119
White Chocolate & Cranberry Tiffin 152

Frosting
Bonfire Cupcakes 140

Fudge
Easy Caramel Pecan Fudge 85
Microwave Maltesers Fudge 97

Fusilli Pasta
One Pot Pizza Pasta 57

G
Garlic & Thyme Baked Camembert 22
Gooey Lemon Pudding 91

Garlic
Cheese Puffs with Fiery Tomato Salsa 13
Chicken Teriyaki 39
Cod Curry 43
Garlic & Thyme Baked Camembert 22
Juicy Chargrilled Lime Chicken 49
Korean Beef 52
One Pot Creamy Garlic Pasta 54
Sweet Potato & Cumin Soup 32

Garlic Infused Olive Oil
Cajun Bean Dip with Cheesy Nachos 5
Garlic & Thyme Baked Camembert 22
Healthy Pitta "Pizzas" 27
Tomato & Mascarpone Risotto 68

Garlic Powder
Tasty Turkey Meatballs 65

Ginger
Cod Curry 43
Korean Beef 52

Golden Syrup
Salted Caramel Choux Buns 107
White Chocolate & Cranberry Tiffin 152

Ground Coriander
Cod Curry 43

Gruyere Cheese
Caramelised Onion & Rosemary Quiche 8

H
Ham & Cheese Pinwheels 24
Healthy Pitta "Pizzas" 27

Ham
Ham & Cheese Pinwheels 24

Honey
Posh Cheese & Onion Tarts 29

Honey Mustard
Juicy Chargrilled Lime Chicken 49
Spicy Sausage Pasta 62

I
Iced Cookies
Blood Spatter Cookies 127

Icing Sugar
Blood Spatter Cookies 127
Bonfire Cupcakes 140
Christmas Pud Teacakes 144
Salted Caramel Choux Buns 107
Red Velvet Cupcakes 119
Victoria Sandwich Cake 114

Italian Salad Dressing
Slow Cooker BBQ Chicken 60
Tomato & Rocket Salad 35

J
Juicy Chargrilled Lime Chicken 49

K
Korean Beef 52

L
Lemon
Blood Spatter Cookies 127
Chorizo Scallops 17
Gooey Lemon Pudding 91

Lettuce
"Eggs & Cheese" 19
Healthy Pitta "Pizzas" 27
Tomato & Mascarpone Risotto 68
Tomato & Rocket Salad 35

Lime
Juicy Chargrilled Lime Chicken 49
Mango & White Chocolate
Cheesecake 94

Linguine Pasta
One Pot Creamy Garlic Pasta 54

M
Mango & White Chocolate
Cheesecake 94

M&M's
Pumpkin Pretzels 138

Malted Milk Powder
White Chocolate & Cranberry Tiffin 152

Maltesers
Microwave Maltesers Fudge 97

Mango
Mango & White Chocolate
Cheesecake 94

Mascarpone Cheese
Tomato & Mascarpone Risotto 68

Matchmakers
Bonfire Cupcakes 140

Mayonnaise
"Eggs & Cheese" 19

Meatballs
Tasty Turkey Meatballs 65

Milk
Bonfire Cupcakes 140
Butterscotch Tart 73
Caramelised Onion & Rosemary Quiche 8
One Pot Creamy Garlic Pasta 54
Salted Caramel Choux Buns 107
Victoria Sandwich Cake 114

Milk Chocolate
Choc Chip Cookie Bars 79
Christmas Tree Brownies 147
Creme Egg Brownies 123
Microwave Maltesers Fudge 97

Minced Beef
Korean Beef 52

Mirin
Chicken Teriyaki 39

Mozzarella Cheese
Cajun Bean Dip with Cheesy Nachos 5
Ham & Cheese Pinwheels 24
Healthy Pitta "Pizzas" 27

Mushrooms
Chicken Teriyaki 39
One Pot Pizza Pasta 57
Posh Cheese & Onion Tarts 29

Mustard
Juicy Chargrilled Lime Chicken 49
Spicy Sausage Pasta 62

N
No Bake Bloody Spider Web
Chocolate Tart 133
Nutella Stuffed Peanut Butter Cookies 100

Nachos
Cajun Bean Dip with Cheesy Nachos 5

Natural Yoghurt
Cod Curry Page 43
Posh Cheese & Onion Tarts 29

Nutella
Nutella Stuffed Peanut Butter Cookies 100

Nuts
Easy Caramel Pecan Fudge 85

O
One Pot Creamy Garlic Pasta 54
One Pot Pizza Pasta 57

Oats
Raspberry Crumble Bars 104

Onion
Caramelised Onion & Rosemary Quiche 8
Cheese Puffs with Fiery Tomato Salsa 13
Chicken Teriyaki 39
Cod Curry 43
Korean Beef 52
One Pot Pizza Pasta 57
Posh Cheese & Onion Tarts 29
Sweet Potato & Cumin Soup 32
Tomato & Rocket Salad 35

Oregano
One Pot Pizza Pasta 57

Oreos
Chocolate Oreo Tart 82
No Bake Bloody Spiderweb
Chocolate Tart 133

P
Posh Cheese & Onion Tarts 29
Pumpkin Pretzels 138

Parsley
Chorizo Scallops 17
Juicy Chargrilled Lime Chicken 49
One Pot Creamy Garlic Pasta 54

Parmesan Cheese
Cheese Puffs with Fiery Tomato Salsa 13
"Eggs & Cheese" 19
One Pot Creamy Garlic Pasta 54
One Pot Pizza Pasta 57
Tasty Turkey Meatballs 65
Tomato & Mascarpone Risotto 68
Tomato & Rocket Salad 35

Pasta
One Pot Creamy Garlic Pasta 54
One Pot Pizza Pasta 57
Spicy Sausage Pasta 62

Pastry
Caramelised Onion & Rosemary Quiche 8
Cheese Puffs with Fiery Tomato Salsa 13
Posh Cheese & Onion Tarts 29
Salted Caramel Choux Buns 107

Peanut Butter
Nutella Stuffed Peanut Butter Cookies 100

Pecans
Easy Caramel Pecan Fudge 85

Pepperoni
One Pot Pizza Pasta 57

Pesto
Creamy Pesto Chicken 47

Pitta Bread
Healthy Pitta "Pizzas" 27

Pizza Dough
Ham & Cheese Pinwheels 24

Pork Sausages
One Pot Pizza Pasta 57

Potato
Sweet Potato & Cumin Soup 32
Tomato & Rocket Salad 35

Pretzels
Pumpkin Pretzels 138

Puff Pastry
Posh Cheese & Onion Tarts 29
Tomato & Rocket Salad 35

Q
Quiche
Caramelised Onion & Rosemary Quiche 8

R
Raspberry Crumble Bars 104
Red Velvet Cupcakes 119

Raspberry Jam
Raspberry Crumble Bars 104

Red Wine
Posh Cheese & Onion Tarts 29

Rice
Chicken Teriyaki 39
Juicy Chargrilled Lime Chicken 49
Korean Beef 52
Tomato & Mascarpone Risotto 68

Risotto
Tomato & Mascarpone Risotto 68

Rocket Lettuce
Healthy Pitta "Pizzas" 27
Tomato & Mascarpone Risotto 68
Tomato & Rocket Salad 35

Rolled Oats
Raspberry Crumble Bars 104

Rosemary
Caramelised Onion & Rosemary Quiche 8

Royal Icing
Blood Spatter Cookies 127

S
Salted Caramel Choux Buns 107
Slow Cooker BBQ Chicken 60
Spicy Sausage Pasta 62
Sweet Potato & Cumin Soup 32

Salad
Healthy Pitta "Pizzas" 27

Salted Caramel
Salted Caramel Choux Buns 107

Sausages
One Pot Pizza Pasta 57
Spicy Sausage Pasta 62

Scallops
Chorizo Scallops 17

Semi Skimmed Milk
Butterscotch Tart 73
One Pot Creamy Garlic Pasta 54

Shortcrust Pastry
Butterscotch Tart 73
Caramelised Onion & Rosemary Quiche 8

Single Cream
Gooey Lemon Pudding 91

Smoked Paprika
Cheese Puffs with Fiery Tomato Salsa 13

Soup
Sweet Potato & Cumin Soup 32

Soy Sauce
Chicken Teriyaki 39
Juicy Chargrilled Lime Chicken 49
Korean Beef 52

Spring Onions
Chicken Teriyaki 39
Korean Beef 52

Star Anise
Posh Cheese & Onion Tarts 29

Strawberry Jam
Victoria Sandwich Cake 114

Sugar Balls
Christmas Pud Teacakes 144
Christmas Tree Brownies 147

Sugar Decorations
Christmas Pud Teacakes 144
Red Velvet Cupcakes 119

Sweet Chilli Sauce
Ham & Cheese Pinwheels 24

T
Tasty Turkey Meatballs 65
Tomato & Mascarpone Risotto 68
Tomato & Rocket Salad 35

Tabasco Sauce
Cheese Puffs with Fiery Tomato Salsa 13

Tart
Butterscotch Tart 73
Chocolate Oreo Tart 82
No Bake Bloody Spiderweb
Chocolate Tart 133
Posh Cheese & Onion Tarts 29

Teacakes
Christmas Pud Teacakes 144

Thyme
Garlic & Thyme Baked Camembert 22
Juicy Chargrilled Lime Chicken 49
Posh Cheese & Onion Tarts 29

Tiffin
White Chocolate & Cranberry Tiffin 152

Tomato
Cajun Bean Dip with Cheesy Nachos 5
Cheese Puffs with Fiery Tomato Salsa 13
Cod Curry 43
Creamy Pesto Chicken 47
Healthy Pitta "Pizzas" 27
Tasty Turkey Meatballs 65
Tomato & Mascarpone Risotto 68
Tomato & Rocket Salad 35

Tomato Purée
Cheese Puffs with Fiery Tomato Salsa 13

Turkey
Tasty Turkey Meatballs 65

U

V
Victoria Sandwich Cake 114

Vanilla Extract
Blood Spatter Cookies 127
Bonfire Cupcakes 140
Butterscotch Tart 73
Choc Chip Cookie Bars 79
Christmas Tree Brownies 147
Creme Egg Brownies 123
Easy Caramel Pecan Fudge 85
Easy One Bowl Brownies 88
Nutella Stuffed Peanut Butter Cookies 100
Red Velvet Cupcakes 119
Victoria Sandwich Cake 114

W
White Chocolate & Cranberry Tiffin 152

White Chocolate
Christmas Tree Brownies 147
Easy Caramel Pecan Fudge 85
Mango & White Chocolate Cheesecake 94
No Bake Bloody Spiderweb
Chocolate Tart 133
Pumpkin Pretzels 138
White Chocolate & Cranberry Tiffin 152

White Wine
Cheese Puffs with Fiery Tomato Salsa 13
Spicy Sausage Pasta 62

White Wine Vinegar
Red Velvet Cupcakes 119

Whole Milk
Bonfire Cupcakes 140

Worcestershire Sauce
Juicy Chargrilled Lime Chicken 49
Slow Cooker BBQ Chicken 60

X

Y
Yoghurt
Cod Curry 43
Posh Cheese & Onion Tarts 29

Z

Printed in Great Britain
by Amazon

28005896R00096